Co-creating Learning and Teaching

Towards Relational Pedagogy in Higher Education

CRITICAL PRACTICE IN HIGHER EDUCATION

Acknowledgements

I would like to thank all the students and staff responsible for many of the inspiring examples contained in this book, and who were willing to share their experiences. I would also like to thank the following people for their encouragement and constructively critical comments: Peter Felten; Joy Jarvis; Julia Morris; Elizabeth Sellers Stanfill; and Karen Smith. Any mistakes or shortcomings are my own. Finally, thank you to Allan, for your love, support and patience while I have been writing this book.

Co-creating Learning and Teaching

Towards Relational Pedagogy in Higher Education

Catherine Bovill

Series Editors: Joy Jarvis and Karen Smith

CRITICAL PRACTICE IN HIGHER EDUCATION

First published in 2020 by Critical Publishing Ltd

British Library Cataloguing in Publication Data
A CIP record for this book is available from the British Library

ISBN: 9781913063818

This book is also available in the following e-book formats:
MOBI ISBN: 9781913063825
EPUB ISBN: 9781913063832
Adobe e-book ISBN: 9781913063849

Cover design by Out of House Limited
Text design by Greensplash Limited
Project Management by Newgen Publishing UK
Printed and bound in the UK by 4edge, Essex

Critical Publishing
3 Connaught Road
St Albans
AL3 5RX

www.criticalpublishing.com

Paper from responsible sources

Contents

Meet the author and series editors

Catherine Bovill is Senior Lecturer in Student Engagement at the Institute for Academic Development (IAD), University of Edinburgh, and Visiting Fellow at the University of Winchester. At the University of Edinburgh she leads a range of strategic student engagement initiatives with a view to supporting culture change towards more engaged forms of learning and teaching. She also leads the programme and course design team in IAD, supporting colleagues across the university in curriculum work. She is a Principal Fellow of the Higher Education Academy and Fellow of the Staff and Educational Development Association. Catherine is an editorial board member for *Teaching in Higher Education* and has been an editor and advisor on several other international journals. She has published and presented internationally on student engagement, students as partners and student–staff co-creation of curricula. She has also contributed to several international and UK change programmes focused on students as partners in curriculum design. In 2019–20 she was a Fulbright Scholar based at Elon University in North Carolina undertaking teaching and research related to student engagement and the role of student–faculty relationships, and was involved in strategic development work.

Joy Jarvis is currently Professor of Educational Practice at the University of Hertfordshire and a UK National Teaching Fellow. She has experience in a wide range of education contexts and works to create effective learning experiences for students and colleagues. She is particularly interested in the professional learning of those engaged in educational practice in higher education settings and has undertaken a range of projects, working with colleagues locally, nationally and internationally, to develop practice in teaching and leadership of teaching. Joy works with doctoral students exploring aspects of educational practice and encourages them to be adventurous in their methodological approaches and to share their findings in a range of contexts to enable practice change.

 **Karen Smith** is Reader in Higher Education in the School of Education at the University of Hertfordshire. She has a strong research interest in transnational education, notably in flying faculty models and is author of the *Transnational Education Toolkit* for the Higher Education Academy. Karen spent many years working on lecturer development programmes and is now the Director of the University of Hertfordshire's Professional Doctorate in Education. She also leads collaborative research and development in her School, where she engages in externally funded research and evaluation and supports the development of scholarly educational practice through practitioner research.

Book summary

Co-creating learning and teaching involves students and staff co-designing curricula or elements of curricula and has been described as one of six key pedagogical ideas in higher education (Ryan and Tilbury, 2013). In this book, I argue that meaningful student engagement through co-creating learning and teaching relies upon good relationships between the teacher and students and between students and their peers. Equally, co-creating learning and teaching contributes to building good relationships. Higher education classrooms (whether face-to-face or online) are a key site of collegial and inclusive possibility that are currently often an under-utilised opportunity to develop relational and co-created learning and teaching. Drawing on literature from school education and higher education, and using a range of examples of co-created learning and teaching from universities internationally, the book highlights the benefits of relational pedagogy and co-creation. Relational pedagogy and co-creation have the potential to lead to more human and engaged forms of learning and teaching in higher education. These are forms of learning and teaching that challenge accepted power relations between teacher and students, enhance inclusivity, increase the relevance of learning to learners and that enable students to practice and develop democratic skills and capabilities they need in their current and future lives.

*Real learning does not happen until students are brought into rela-
tionship with the teacher, with each other, and with the subject.
We cannot learn deeply and well until a community of learning is
created in the classroom.*

(Palmer, 1983, p xvi)

Relational pedagogy as the foundation for co-creating learning and teaching

The higher education (HE) environment today is highly complex. Increasing numbers of students are coming to university to study at the same time that resources are redu-cing in many contexts, placing growing pressure on institutions that are attempting to maintain or enhance the quality of what they offer. Universities are also challenged to meet the needs of an increasingly diverse range of students. Governments around the world have influenced a neoliberal agenda to take hold in universities, where business and management models now dominate HE, with emphasis placed on efficiency and outcome measures. In the UK, this neoliberal agenda has led to the introduction of the Teaching Excellence Framework (TEF) in 2017 – to mirror the existing Research Excellence Framework (REF): tools that aim to measure teaching and research per-formance respectively. However, there are widespread concerns that the metrics being used to calculate teaching excellence are unsuitable (Cuffe, 2019; Kandiko Howson, 2016).

With the massification of HE, all staff in HE institutions face the challenge of how they can support students to feel that they belong and are valued. How can we get to know students when student numbers are so high and when we regularly teach students in large classes? The managerial and economic priorities of many universities which create large classes and a reliance on transactional language to describe educa-tion lead to a tension for many staff who aim to adopt more personal approaches to teaching and supporting students. Biesta critiques the current situation and argues:

To think of education as an economic transaction, as a process of meeting the needs of the learner – something that is made possible by the new language of learning – is therefore first of all problematic because it misconstrues both the role of the learner and the role of the educational

1

professional in the educational relationship. It forgets that a major reason for engaging in educa-
tion is precisely to find out what it is that one actually wants or needs. It also forgets that educa-
tional professionals have a crucial role to play in the process of needs definition, because a major
part of their professional expertise lies precisely there; a role that precisely distinguishes them
from shop assistants whose only task it is to deliver the goods to the customer.

(Biesta, 2006, p 22)

There are encouraging signs that some people are taking a different, more social, human and nurturing approach within HE. In this book, I explore some exciting alternatives to an impersonal customer-focused version of HE. Co-creating learning and teaching is becoming more widespread across the world and the beneficial outcomes that are being demonstrated are compelling (Bovill, 2019b; Cook-Sather et al, 2014; Mercer-Mapstone et al, 2017). Co-creation of learning and teaching is where students and staff share decision-making about the design of whole curricula or elements of curricula, and this approach has been described as one of six key pedagogical ideas in HE (Ryan and Tilbury, 2013). Alongside co-creation, a growing number of teachers are excited by the possibilities of teaching in ways that help to build meaningful relationships between staff and students.

This brings me to the two key arguments I make in this book.

1. There is a two-way, mutually reinforcing connection between co-creating learning and teaching and positive relationships. You need positive relationships between teacher and students, and between students and their peers, in order to establish the trust necessary for co-creating learning and teaching. And through co-creating learning and teaching – involving shared decision-making, shared responsibility and negotiation of learning and teaching – teachers and students, and students and their peers, form deep, meaningful relationships;

2. HE classrooms (whether face-to-face or online) – which are one of the most common places that staff and students meet in universities – are a key site of collegial and inclusive possibility that are currently often an under-used opportunity for relational pedagogy and co-creation.

Currently the ideas within my first argument tend to form two distinct bodies of research literature – developing co-creation of learning and teaching, and relational pedagogy. This book attempts to draw these ideas together. The second argument is largely absent from the expanding literature on partnership, co-creation and relational pedagogy. Drawing on literature from school education and HE, and using examples of co-created learning and teaching from universities, the book highlights the benefits of classroom-level, relational pedagogy and co-creation, including:

- » development of more human and engaged forms of learning and teaching;
- » enhanced learning and positive outcomes for students;
- » greater inclusivity;
- » increased relevance of learning to students;
- » enabling students to practise and develop democratic skills and capabilities.

What are relational pedagogy and co-creation?

I explain what is meant by relational pedagogy and co-creation in the next sections and throughout the rest of the book.

Relational pedagogy

Relational pedagogy puts relationships at the heart of teaching and emphasises that a meaningful connection needs to be established between teacher and students as well as between students and their peers, if effective learning is to take place. Yet, establishing trust between staff and students in the classroom can be challenging where many current practices alienate students (Mann, 2001). Indeed, before students are able to trust or respect teachers, teachers need to build good relationships and demonstrate that they care about students through effective communication of an interest in, respect for, and belief in students and their capabilities.

Noddings (2010, p vii) argues that *'reactions of students invited into a caring relation often include increased interest in the subject matter...; enhanced self-esteem...; and concern for others'*. How can we expect to have positive learning and teaching experiences without mutual trust or respect? Plevin (2017) goes on to argue that there are two essential factors for building positive relationships:

1. showing students that we care;
2. communicating frequently with students.

Relational pedagogy is explored in more depth in Chapter 2.

Co-creation of learning and teaching

Let us now consider what is meant by co-creation of learning and teaching. In work I conducted with colleagues from the UK, USA and Ireland, we defined co-creation as occurring 'when staff and students work collaboratively with one another to create components of curricula and/or pedagogical approaches' (Bovill et al, 2016, p 196). Co-creation recognises that students have valuable perspectives and contributions to bring to teaching and learning (Cook-Sather et al, 2014), and implies deeper engagement – such as shared decision-making – than might be found in common forms of active learning and interaction (Bovill, 2019b). While the term co-creation has been used quite widely in business and management literature, and the term participatory co-design is also considered a related term – in these cases there is more of a focus on co-creation with employers or user-testing in marketing of new goods or technology (see for example, Di Salvo et al, 2017).

Engaging students deeply in discussions about learning and teaching enhances understanding of learning and teaching processes, increases motivation and enhances the learning and teaching experiences – for students and teachers (Cook-Sather et al, 2014). Co-creation also leads to increases in students' academic performance and grades, a greater sense of belonging and enhanced relationships and trust between students and staff, and between students and their peers (Cook-Sather et al, 2014; Mercer-Mapstone et al, 2017). Cook-Sather, interviewed in 2015 at Uppsala University (cited in Barrineau et al, 2019, p 174), explains the importance of discussing with students the value of students' perspectives. She envisages having a conversation with students where she might say:

I value your perspectives on what learning is like in my classroom, I can't know that, I can only know what it's like to teach in this classroom but only you know what it is like to learn in this classroom. So you have a perspective that I don't have and that I would benefit from hearing so that I can make sure that the learning is the best experience that it can be for you.

She goes on to add:

And again it isn't about what students like – it's about what best facilitates their learning, and that distinction I think is really key. Because the what students like and don't like plays into the consumer model of education... but analysing what makes for good learning, that's a very different conversation.

Many different forms of co-creation exist, from involving a small number of students in co-designing the entire curriculum or selecting a course text book as part of a curriculum planning group, to involvement of a whole class of students in creating their own essay titles or designing their own course evaluation (Bovill et al, 2010; Cook-Sather et al, 2014; Mihans et al, 2008). More examples of co-creation are explored in Chapters 3 and 4.

Are these approaches new?

There has been increasing interest in co-creation of, and *students as partners* in, learning and teaching across universities internationally in the last ten years (Bovill, 2013; Cook-Sather et al, 2014; Healey et al, 2014), and in relational pedagogy in schools over the last 20 years (Bingham and Sidorkin, 2010; Noddings, 1992 and 2010). We are also witnessing growing interest in the importance of relationships in HE (Beard et al, 2007; Felten, 2017; Felten and Lambert, 2020; Quinlan, 2016; Schwartz, 2019).

Co-creation and relational pedagogy draw upon some common theoretical frameworks and authors. There is a long history highlighting the importance of relations going back to Aristotle (Bingham and Sidorkin, 2010), and in the early twentieth century, Dewey argued for more progressive, democratic classrooms and school environments (Dewey, 1916). Dewey's work influenced many scholars and students who followed. Heidegger in 1968 released *What Is Called Thinking?*, in which he challenged ideas of the teacher–student relationship, suggesting that more freedom and openness was needed. Rogers's book *The Freedom to Learn*, published in 1969, returned to many ideas that Dewey proposed, including calls for students to participate more fully in co-designing learning processes. In the 1970s, there were several robust critiques of formal schooling including Illich's book *Deschooling Society* and Willis' book *Learning to Labour*. Also in the 1970s, Paulo Friere's *Pedagogy of the Oppressed* proposed that popular education was of more value to people than formal education. Popular education highlights the everyday needs of learners and enables them to become conscious of their own subordinate position in society in order to identify practical and radical solutions to overcome their oppression. Friere's work was particularly influential in community and adult education globally but has also influenced many teachers working in schools and universities.

In the 1980s, we saw the rise of *critical pedagogy* (Giroux, 1983), which focused on students and staff negotiating and collaborating to co-create new forms of knowledge from their own experiences to challenge existing views of the world (Darder et al, 2013). Many authors built on these ideas and those of Rogers to argue that students should share the responsibility for curriculum planning (Aronowitz, 1981; Boomer, 1982 and 1992; Bovill, 2009; Bron, Bovill, Van Vliet and Veugelers, 2016; Bron et al, 2016 and 2018; hooks, 1994; Pinar, 1981). It was also in the 1980s that Noddings brought the idea of relational approaches into mainstream school education discourse in the USA (Noddings, 1984). From the 1970s onwards, we also saw growing research evidence in HE demonstrating the benefits of student–staff and student–student relationships (Lamport, 1993; Mayhew et al, 2016).

However, despite this rich evidence base supporting more relational forms of education, Apple (1981, p 115) argues *'we are willing to prepare students to assume only some responsibility for their own learning'*. Apple's words, nearly 40 years ago, suggest that we face some challenges with co-creation and relational pedagogy in bridging the gap between espoused ideals and actual practice.

Why pursue these approaches?

As we consider the rising interest in relational pedagogy and co-creation of learning and teaching, *'it is vital to think through carefully about your reasons for student engagement and how the "why" of participation is communicated to students'* (Barrineau et al 2019, p 172). Without explicitly considering our rationales for adopting relational approaches and discussing these motivations with students, we miss opportunities to build trust through enhancing transparency and finding out how our motivations match (or not) students' motivations for engagement.

There are several key rationales that teachers regularly give for pursuing co-creation. For some, they have been keen to try a new, more engaging approach, when a course has been receiving poor student feedback. Sometimes, teachers have been opportunistic in gaining modest funding to help in supporting this kind of pedagogical enhancement, or they have used institutional structural or procedural changes, such as changing the credit weighting of modules, to try implementing a new co-creation approach. Universities are often keen to enhance student experience and satisfaction levels measured in large-scale surveys such as the UK National Student Survey (NSS) and this can lead teachers to experiment with new ways of engaging students. Some colleagues are influenced by the beneficial outcomes from relational pedagogy and co-creation. Other colleagues are coming to recognise that including students more meaningfully in negotiating learning and teaching enables us to benefit from the variety of valuable perspectives that students bring to the learning process. There is another group of staff who are influenced by authors such as Friere, Giroux, hooks and Rogers who argue that education is political, and should be relational, emancipatory, and thereby challenge hegemonic structures and processes to ensure that students become empowered, active citizens. For this group of staff, co-creation is a way of democratising the classroom and enabling students to engage in negotiation and shared decision-making.

Bron and Veugelers (2014) in the Netherlands outlined five arguments for involving school pupils in co-creating learning and teaching:

1. the normative argument – students *should* have a say in designing their own education;

2. the developmental argument – students are capable of co-designing the curriculum;

3. the political argument – students are not an homogenous group, and we must include diverse student voices;

4. the educational argument – students will learn useful knowledge and negotiation skills through co-creation;

5. the relevance argument – when students influence the curriculum through co-creation, it makes the curriculum more relevant and engaging.

All of these arguments can be relatively easily translated into the HE setting. In addition, many of the rationales for co-creating learning and teaching overlap with those given for pursuing relational pedagogy, not least a growing sense of disenfranchisement with a marketised educational environment, associated with a lack of connection between staff and students, and an ineffectiveness in creating a sense of belonging (Bovill, 2019c; Cook-Sather and Felten, 2017).

Critical issues

Let's hear from students why they want to be involved

Barrineau et al (2019) report that students provide many reasons for wanting to become more deeply engaged in their learning:

» they find it fun;

» students learn more by explaining things to other students;

» student involvement in making decisions about courses helps them see how they have a role in learning – and the associated freedom and responsibility;

» students adopt deeper approaches to learning;

» students can gain self-confidence by sharing difficult problems and questions with peers and realising they are not the only one struggling, as well as benefitting from shared perspectives;

» sharing students' different perspectives helps teachers understand how students experience teaching;

→

» students gain an understanding of course design choices made by teachers through working together;

» students co-creating learning and teaching with teachers experience new understandings of learning and teaching that make it hard to go back to previous non-collaborative forms of education.

Chapter outlines

The themes presented so far are explored further in the rest of this book.

Chapter 2, 'Relationships in learning and teaching', examines and critiques the research that demonstrates how successful learning outcomes are the result of positive relationships between teacher and students, and between students and their peers. The concept of relational pedagogy is explored, and readers are provided with examples of how relationships influence student engagement, belonging and the culture of the classroom.

Chapter 3, 'Co-creating learning and teaching', provides a critique of the research on student engagement, active learning, partnership and co-creating learning and teaching. Attention is drawn to the vast array of practice that is covered by each of these concepts, and some useful models and ways of conceptualising co-creation are presented as well as evidence of the benefits and challenges of co-creation.

In Chapter 4, 'Towards relational pedagogy in higher education', the concepts of relational pedagogy and co-creating learning and teaching are drawn together. Positive relationships are considered to be foundational to co-creating learning and teaching, as well as being an outcome from co-creation. You are encouraged to consider each meeting with a new class of students as an opportunity to create meaningful relationships and to co-create learning and teaching – currently, these early teaching encounters are often missed opportunities.

Chapter 5, 'What does this mean for my teaching practice?', draws upon the previous chapters to propose a range of questions for teachers to consider in their own practice, whatever the context in which you are working. These questions are aimed at all teachers, but acknowledge that some readers may be relatively new to teaching in HE. You are encouraged to consider teaching practices that involve relational connections with students, and that explore the possibilities of co-creating learning and teaching.

In Chapter 6, 'Conclusions', I synthesise the implications from the previous chapters including a call for culture change towards more relational and co-creation approaches.

Summary

- Co-creating learning and teaching involves staff and students actively co-designing and negotiating elements of the curriculum.

- Relational pedagogy refers to the need to establish a meaningful connection between teacher and students as well as between students and their peers if trust is to be established and effective learning is to take place.

- I propose that relational pedagogy is the foundation for co-creation of learning and teaching as well as an outcome of co-creation.

- Co-creation and relational pedagogy are not new ideas and many previous authors have described concepts that relate to these ideas.

- There are many different rationales given for pursuing co-creation and relational pedagogy.

Useful texts

Bingham, C and Sidorkin, A M (2010) Introduction. In Bingham, C and Sidorkin, A M (eds) *No Education Without Relation.* New York: Peter Lang Publishing.

An introduction to the idea of relational pedagogy.

Cook-Sather, A, Bovill, C and Felten, P (2014) *Engaging Students as Partners in Learning and Teaching: A Guide for Faculty.* San Francisco: Jossey Bass.

Written specifically to introduce staff to the idea of working in partnership with students in learning and teaching. Despite using the term partnership, it suggests different degrees of partnership with a lot of overlap with the idea of co-creation.

Teaching and learning are relational activities. We must be in a relationship with each other for learning to happen.

(Werder et al, 2010, p 28)

Is something missing in our current teaching?

Mayhew et al (2016, p 592) argue that:

Good teaching matters. It really matters... good teaching is the primary means through which institutions affect students. In addition, high-quality instruction was generally more effective in promoting the learning, cognitive, and educational attainment outcomes of students from historically underserved populations than those from majority groups. Importantly, these practices also promote desired outcomes for all students.

Although we have some rich research about how students learn, capturing and describing what is taking place during the process of learning proves difficult. This is not really surprising if we recognise that *'education is ultimately and immediately about an encounter between persons'* (Fielding, 1999, p 22), and encounters are not easy to measure, judge or capture.

Critical issues

Capturing the essence of teaching and learning

How many books or articles have you read where someone describes in detail the processes taking place when teaching and learning happen? The following are writing extracts that manage to capture a sense of some of the processes taking place in teaching. What stands out to me in these examples is the importance of relationships and emotions in teaching and learning.

→

A teaching approach at The Evergreen State College, Washington, USA

Students in one Evergreen class decided to give each member 10 beans, with the idea being that a bean be surrendered for each contribution to the discussion as a way of monitoring one another's participation. Once a student's 10 beans were gone, they couldn't contribute any more that day. The day we observed, the class was abuzz with different groups reporting on their discussion. Some talked straight from the assigned readings, others incorporated experiences and information from other classes. One woman, who already offered a number of pithy observations, prefaces her next comment with, 'My beans are almost up now'. Another who said relatively little offers up some of her beans. Still another less talkative student opens with 'I had better use up some of my beans....' This goes on for more than 90 minutes. Close to the ending time, the faculty member says, 'I see people packing up; my sense is that we're done.' Two students voice their objection, 'No let's hear from the last group.' The last group briefly summarizes their work. The faculty member then asks, 'How did we do on our process?' One student tells another, 'You seemed quiet today.' The student responds saying she felt that she talked too much last week and was trying to let others respond today. Another student comments that he 'liked the challenge of today's discussion... I don't think we needed the beans today.' By the end of the class almost everyone has contributed at least once.

(Kuh et al, 2005, p 71)

Giving feedback to, and receiving feedback from, a student

A few years ago, a student had given me an extensive journal and asked me to make comments. I spent several hours with the journal, making long remarks in the margins and asking questions about what he had written. His next journal entry, which he also gave to me, was sharp and abrupt. He resented my comments. I was hurt and angry. I returned his short journal entry with no comments, or perhaps an equally short comment, I cannot recall that now. That evening, my response to him did not sit well with me. I wrote him a rather long note in which I explained my reasons for my comments – I was interested in what he wrote, I felt I had something to say about it. I also told him that I was upset by his sharp reply, and I speculated on why I had this reaction. My note was authentic and it served to reconnect me with the student. He and I still correspond regularly.

(Cranton, 2001, p 79)

Some of the difficulty in trying to measure, or capture the essence of, teaching and learning arises from the variety of ways in which these concepts are defined. We still regularly see references to teaching *delivery*, as if teaching a subject can be considered analogous to pizza delivery. Fielding (1999, p 23) reacts strongly to this idea:

talk of delivering the curriculum is disgusting and dishonest: disgusting because it replaces the ethically and experientially nuanced language of learning with the monologic, the mechanistic, and the myopic; dishonest because learning cannot be sensibly conceived of in this way and therefore cannot be accomplished in this way either.

Manor et al (2010, p 10) also draw attention to the problem with considering teaching as delivery:

the assumption that professors possess all the course-related knowledge and that students have none contributes to a fundamental misunderstanding of what it means to learn – that learning essentially is the transfer of knowledge, a finite set of facts, from professor to student, rather than a process that allows examination and making meaning from knowledge.

Giroux coined the term *critical pedagogy* for a major critique of existing approaches to teaching. Giroux and others were making the case for more freedom for students to make choices and decisions about their own learning, a more dialogic student–teacher relationship, and a shift to viewing the learner as a competent contributor to education (Bovill, 2013; Giroux, 1983). Giroux and other key authors such as hooks and Rogers placed emphasis on building genuine relationships between teacher and students as well as recognising that learning is a social experience and, therefore, relationships between students and their peers also matter. Romano (2010) argues in terms of school education that teachers' preparation often overlooks the quality of relationships with students that are needed for engagement and co-construction of knowledge. This is also the case in many professional development programmes for teachers in HE, where relationships, emotions and relational teaching are not frequently prioritised (Quinlan, 2016).

Relationships in teaching and learning in HE

Within HE, there is a substantial body of research that demonstrates the positive benefits of student–staff relationships. Much of this has come from large-scale and sustained work in the United States since the 1970s and 1980s. This research demonstrates that student–teacher interaction both inside and outside the classroom is important (Kuh and Huh, 2001; Mayhew et al, 2016). Frequent and high-quality student–teacher interaction has been linked to: improvements in students' academic grades; students having higher educational aspirations; greater learner autonomy and confidence; enhanced student satisfaction, engagement and motivation; and increased personal and intellectual development (see for example Astin, 1977; Brownell and Swaner, 2010; Chickering and Gamson, 1987; Cuseo, 2007; Komarraju et al, 2010; Kuh and Hu, 2001; Lamport, 1993; Mayhew et al, 2016; Pascarella and Terenzini, 1978 and 2005). Lamport cites evidence that shows *'faculty members are the prime agents of personal and intellectual influence in the lives of students'* (Lamport, 1993, p 975) and teacher attitudes are considered to be a key factor in creating positive learning environments that include positive relationships with students (Scheck and Bizio, 1977; Theophilides and Terenzini, 1981). Some researchers have even identified a range of staff characteristics – including staff being warm and informal, friendly, genuine, respectful and understanding – that are linked to the development of positive teacher–student relationships (Long, 1977; Theophilides and Terenzini, 1981).

When staff make an effort to learn students' names, this communicates to students that staff care about them and do not just see them as an anonymous student in a large crowd of students (Thomas, 2012), because as Kuh et al (2005, p 288) warn, *'as institutions increase in size, it becomes easy to be anonymous'*. At Arizona State University, they found that using *name tents* in large classes demonstrated statistically significant results in enhancing student motivation and learning, including making it more likely they would ask staff for help (Cooper et al, 2017). What is particularly interesting about this work is that staff do not need to actually remember students' names; it appears that teachers making the effort to call students by their name wherever possible demonstrates to students that teachers care enough to try to learn their names.

De Los Reyes (2002, p 41) reports how a student described her experience of classes in college:

I notice in a lot of my classes we write and the teacher speaks. But I found that a lot of the classes that I take we get into a circle, like my psychology or women's studies classes. I try to stay within those classes, because I don't feel so intimidated… Every semester I try to take classes that are like that, [rather than] going to class and listening to the teacher go on and on when she/he doesn't even know your name.

Critical issues

Factors leading to positive student outcomes in HE

In 1987, Chickering and Gamson drew upon the robust and large-scale research into student learning and teaching at university to summarise key factors leading to positive student outcomes. This list of principles remains influential.

→

Seven principles for good practice in undergraduate education

Good practice in undergraduate education:

1. *encourages contacts between students and faculty;*

2. *develops reciprocity and cooperation between students;*

3. *uses active learning techniques;*

4. *gives prompt feedback;*

5. *emphasises time on task;*

6. *communicates high expectations;*

7. *respects diverse talents and ways of working.*

(Chickering and Gamson, 1987, p 3)

Principles 1, 2 and 3 are perhaps most closely linked to the importance of developing good relationships between teacher and students, and between students and students.

High impact practices

In 2006, George Kuh introduced the concept of 'high impact practices' (HIPs) to denote experiences with robust evidence that they contribute to positive student outcomes. The 11 identified HIPs are:

1. *first-year experiences;*

2. *common intellectual experiences;*

3. *learning communities;*

4. *writing-intensive courses;*

5. *collaborative assignments and projects;*

6. *undergraduate research;*

7. *diversity/global learning;*

8. *e-portfolios;*

→

> *9. service learning, community-based learning;*
>
> *10. internships;*
>
> *11. capstone courses and projects.*
>
> (Kuh et al, 2017)
>
> Some HIPs appear, at first glance, to specifically require, and contribute to building, positive relationships (eg 3, 5, 6 and 9). But most of these practices are associated with strong relationships, and perhaps this is one factor contributing to their high impact. There is increasing evidence that where students experience multiple and connected HIPs, students experience particularly impressive benefits (Browner and Swanell, 2010).

Many authors outline the benefits of student relationships with their peers (Astin, 1993; Chickering and Gamson, 1987; Kuh et al, 2005; Mayhew et al, 2016; Pascarella and Terenzini, 2005; Thomas, 2012). We also need to acknowledge that within any learning environment, the quality of student–teacher interaction is likely to have a significant influence on the nature of the student–student interaction that is facilitated during class. Manor et al (2010, p 7) ask *'can you imagine a classroom where students take responsibility for each other in addition to just themselves? Can you imagine how much more we would learn, how much we would benefit?'* We need to ensure that we are building in opportunities for students to connect meaningfully with other students in our face-to-face and online classes.

The evidence highlights the importance of building teacher–student and student–student relationships inside *and* outside the classroom, but I have emphasised relationships inside the classroom as these are considered the most powerful for enhancing learning and are most relevant to the focus of this book.

The role of belonging and emotions

Thomas (2012, p 12) argued that research evidence highlighted *'the importance of students having a strong sense of belonging in HE, which is the result of engagement, and that this is most effectively nurtured through mainstream activities with an overt academic purpose that all students participate in'*. Much of this sense of belonging is developed through strong relationships and meaningful interactions between teacher and students and between students and their peers (Carruthers Thomas, 2019; Thomas, 2012).

Belonging is complex and multifaceted, and institutions create conditions in which some students find it easier to belong than others. The UK HE sector discourse *'positions those who are perceived as "not belonging" as problematic rather than the reductive nature of the narrative itself* (Carruthers Thomas, 2019, p 16). As Yahinaaw (2019, p 8), an indigenous student, states: *'I want to engage in partnerships where I can bring myself and be myself*. Yet too often students feel that they have to hide their true identity in order to feel accepted, valued and included as part of communities on campus. Relationships enhance connectedness with others, but Thomas (2012) reminds us that each of us may have a different level of need to belong and to connect with others, something we should be mindful of when trying to enhance the positive relationships we have with students. Nevertheless, Quinlan (2016, p 106) claims that *'students may come to the same lecture halls several times a week for a whole term and never actually meet anyone else in their class'*. This surely is unacceptable, and highlights the need for teachers to provide opportunities for paired and small group learning, even in large classes.

Thomas (2012) and Mayhew et al (2016) both argue that teachers play a key role in shaping belonging as well as student outcomes – in other words, teachers' actions in classrooms *'ensure all students benefit'* (Thomas, 2012, p 17). This resonates with my argument; when teachers build relationships and co-create learning and teaching with a whole class of students online or face-to-face, they have the potential to build powerful and inclusive learning environments that can lead to positive outcomes for all students (Bovill, 2019b).

Another concept connected to positive relationships is that of emotion within learning and teaching. Quinlan (2016, p 102) argues *'emotion matters in higher education because education is relational, and emotions are central to relationships'*. Indeed, there is growing interest in the role of positive relationships and emotions in HE (Beard et al, 2007; Felten, 2017; Felten and Lambert, 2020; Quinlan, 2016; Schwartz, 2019). Yet despite this growth of interest, emotions have tended to be overlooked in much writing about learning and teaching (Quinlan, 2016) and about partnerships (Felten, 2017). Writing specifically about the rise in recent student–staff partnership work (and directly related to co-creation), Felten (2017, p 2) highlights that *'emotion clearly is a component of student-faculty partnerships, yet academic customs—including our scholarly forms of writing—privilege the rational. That narrow focus obscures important aspects of partnership'*.

He goes on to argue that *'we cannot understand the interactions and relationships between individuals in partnerships without attending to emotions... focusing on the emotional dimensions of partnerships will shine new light on the dynamic processes and the powerful outcomes of this work'* (p 3).

Ecclestone and Hayes (2019) provide a robust critique of the trend towards therapeutic education, which they describe as the vast increase in resources and attention paid to popular therapy for mental health, viewing students as vulnerable, and associated attention paid to emotions and relationships. They argue that this trend risks lowering expectations of students, trivialises serious mental illness and overlooks the important place of knowledge in education. So it is important to note that scholars of student–teacher relationships, relational pedagogy and co-creation in fact argue for raising expectations of students (Bovill et al, 2011; Felten et al, 2016; Quinlan, 2016), and knowledge remains a key aspect of the curriculum which students are being invited to co-create (Bovill and Woolmer, 2019). Beard et al (2007, p 236) also helpfully remind us that *'the question is not whether emotion should be introduced into the curriculum… the affective and embodied are already aspects of all pedagogical encounters but… in higher education, in particular, emotion is rarely acknowledged'*.

Relational pedagogy in school education

The importance of relationships in teaching and learning is discussed in school education literature, which often cites the term *relational pedagogy*, first introduced by Nel Noddings (Bingham and Sidorkin, 2010). Romano (2010) argues that there are different ways in which relational pedagogy is described but most definitions focus on the importance of relationships between students and teacher, and students and their peers, developing meaningful connections in order for effective learning to take place. Kostenius and Bergmark (2016) found that schoolchildren, involved in a health and wellbeing project, felt appreciated, listened to and cared for by teachers and peers, and that this enhanced their sense of well-being. These healthy teacher–student and student–student relationships, according to Fisher et al (2018), require respect, honesty, trust and communication, and for many teachers this requires a change in the way they normally teach.

Damon (2018, p 28) argues that *'a relational teacher gauges how to balance being professional with being human. Students can smell insincerity with acuity'*. Relationships need to be authentic, based on trust, and involve teachers in demonstrating that they care about students and believe in their capabilities. In relational pedagogy, the dialogue which is enabled between everyone in the class can support exploration and co-construction of knowledge: '*a relational approach argues that knowing is some-thing people develop as they have experiences with each other and the world around them*' (Thayer-Bacon, 2010, p 166). This contrasts distinctly with the idea of teaching delivery.

Within schools, relational pedagogy changes what is possible, '*teachers with relationships at the core of their practice can go into virtually any classroom in any school, and succeed with even the most belligerent, difficult students*' (Plevin, 2017, p 11). Similarly, relational pedagogy is considered to be an approach that can be restorative within schools where there has been violence or entrenched behavioural problems (McCluskey, 2018). Although this focus on classroom management and restorative practice may seem less relevant within HE, it is still worth highlighting that HE teachers who place relationships at the core of their practice are likely to find that students become more engaged and motivated, with associated positive outcomes. Biesta et al (2010) go further in suggesting that relational pedagogy creates an ideal notion of education, requiring and practising democratic relationships within learning and teaching.

Critical questions for practice

What does it mean to create positive relationships with students?

Julie had... a traumatic experience. Her grandmother had passed away. She had been very close to her grandmother when she was a child... Julie spent a week away from college to attend the funeral and to be with her family... she did not inform her professors about her absence until after she returned to college. Julie was quite apprehensive... she did not want to be seen as making excuses for the coursework she had missed, and she felt a bit guilty for not contacting her instructors earlier. But at the same time, she wanted to let her professors know that she had been absent for a very legitimate reason... On the first day of her return, she approached her English professor after class. She told the professor why she had not attended the previous week's classes. The professor acted in a very sympathetic manner. She did not say a word to Julie about the absence itself, not a word about Julie's classwork. Rather, she asked if Julie had been close to her grandmother and Julie answered yes... Julie and her English professor stood at the front of an empty classroom. 'If there is any-thing I can do for you,' the professor said, 'please let me know'... Julie contrasts this

→

first reception to a different sort that she faced upon explaining her absence to her history professor. The history professor said, 'Well you know that you missed last week's quiz, don't you?' 'Yes' Julie responded. 'Well you're going to have to make that up within two days.' 'All right', Julie said. 'And', her professor continued, 'I'll need to have a written verification of your absence. I'll need that note before you can actually take the makeup quiz. That's my policy for every student no matter how extenuating the circumstances'... [Julie reflected]... As my history teacher was talking, I became so angry with her for ignoring my feelings, for being so unsympathetic. She lost all credibility in my view. After that, I refused to work hard in that class. She lost her authority as a teacher over me.

(Bingham, 2010, pp 24–5)

» Consider the student's experience related by Bingham. What are your first reactions to this story?

» Which teacher's response do you think would have been closest to how you might have responded? Why?

Julie's reflections on how the history teacher's response influences her future studying demonstrates the impact that teacher–student interactions can have. Think about ways in which you might adapt the way you would respond in situations like this to balance programme regulations and requirements with showing your support for students' welfare and learning.

Why have we been reluctant to focus on relationships?

If we take the research from HE and school education that has been presented so far, there is robust evidence of the benefits of positive student–teacher and student–student relationships. What can seem puzzling is why we do not practise evidence-based teaching – in other words, we often continue to teach in universities in ways that do not prioritise establishing and developing trusting relationships.

In many universities, the lower status of teaching compared to research, and a lack of awareness by teachers of the robust research literature on university teaching, create barriers to implementing relational teaching. For colleagues in UK HE, this situation is exacerbated by much of the research on relationships originating in the USA and in the school education sector. If professional development for teachers in HE does not highlight the key role of relationships in teaching and learning, newer staff are not likely to hear about or prioritise the role of relationships in teaching unless they have a strong leaning towards relational approaches in other aspects of their lives. Even where teachers are aware of the important role of positive relationships in improved student outcomes, they may be reluctant to change their practice if building relationships with students each time they meet a new class is considered more demanding than other forms of teaching. Staff may also be unaware that relational pedagogy can be more rewarding.

As stated earlier, relational approaches are difficult to capture. '*As we make the transition from old ways of thinking toward a pedagogy based in reciprocal relationships, a truly deep listening, and a view of the student as powerful and capable, we find that we lack the words to describe this more democratic, open interdependence among faculty and students*' (Drummond and Owens, 2010, p 163). And yet, unless we can explain what we mean by relational pedagogy, with practical examples of some approaches to use in class, and evidence of its impact, some staff are likely to be unwilling, or will not know how, to take the first steps in relational teaching.

Relational teaching relies on acknowledging and welcoming student and staff emotions, interests and personal stories, so it is perhaps not surprising that some parts of HE resist this as inappropriate, unscientific or not serious enough. MacFarlane (2004, p 122) reported in his work that some academics '*were less enthusiastic about bringing personal or emotional issues into the classroom… for these individuals, there is a firm line between the 'academic' and the 'personal' and a suitable distance should be maintained between the two'.*

In addition, there was a questioning of '*whether lecturers are sufficiently equipped to deal with the consequences of encouraging students to engage emotionally as well as intellectually*' (MacFarlane, 2004, p 122).

Any discussion of staff–student relationships and student–student relationships tends to evoke a snigger or more serious concerns from some colleagues about inappropriate relationships. In advocating for positive relationships, how do we ensure that we maintain professional boundaries? This is a question I have been asked many times by colleagues who are concerned that either students will want to become their best friend, will think they can phone them at home over the weekend, or that they might misconstrue friendliness for interest in developing romantic or sexual relationships. However, these queries imply a misunderstanding of the kinds of collegial relationships I am advocating for in learning and teaching. Yes, I am advocating for closer relationships in which we get to know students, their interests, experiences, knowledge and talents better than we do within our current teaching practice (and that we are prepared to reciprocate in letting students get to know something of our backgrounds). However, I am not advocating that we lose our professionalism. It is possible to be both professional and approachable, to have appropriate boundaries and to also share some personal stories and experiences to help build mutual trust and respect. There will always be a very small number of staff and students who do not judge professional boundaries well. This will be the case whether we proceed with relational teaching or with more common teaching delivery. I believe the evidence demonstrating the positive impacts of relational teaching are compelling enough that we should be ensuring relational teaching is at the heart of HE. But to support more relational teaching, we need to provide good professional development for staff to work through legitimate concerns such as this.

Another key factor is that building deep connections and relationships takes time. Teachers cannot expect students to trust them immediately but, rather, good relationships require the building of rapport, respect and trust over time. Plevin (2017, p 10) describes a school teacher who had not taken time to get to know his students and was struggling with pupils' behaviour: *'because they didn't know him they could neither trust him nor respect him. How can you really trust someone you don't know?'* Once teachers start to realise the possible benefits of student–teacher and student–student relationships, the question might change to how a teacher can afford *not to* invest the time to build relationships in learning and teaching.

There is also an emancipatory emphasis within much of the critical pedagogy; feminist pedagogy and student voice literature has informed many of the calls for more relational pedagogy (Fielding, 1999; Rogers and Freiberg, 1994; Shrewsbury, 1987), and this language of emancipation is threatening to teachers' position of privilege, and for others it may feel a step too far. And yet as Shor (1992, p 12) argues, '*a curriculum that does not challenge the standard syllabus and conditions in society informs students that knowledge and the world are fixed and are fine the way they are, with no role for students to play in transforming them, and no need for change*'. We need to challenge the idea that knowledge and curricula are neutral. Shor (1992, p 14) highlights the importance of questioning the assumptions behind our teaching, by asking: *Whose history and literature is taught and whose is ignored? Which groups are included and which left out of the reading list or text? From whose point of view is the past and present examined? Which themes are emphasized and which not? Is the curriculum balanced and multicultural... or is it traditionally male-oriented and Eurocentric? Do students read about Columbus from the point of view of the Arawak people he conquered or only from the point of view of the Europeans he led into conquest? Do science classes investigate the biochemistry of the students' lives, like the nutritional value of the school lunch or the potential toxins in the local air, water, and land, or do they only talk abstractly about photosynthesis?*

Another barrier to relational pedagogy may be the size of some classes in schools and universities. Thayer-Bacon (2010) argues that the larger the number of students, the harder it is to establish caring relationships between teacher and students, but also between students and their peers.

By now, you may be wondering how we can overcome some of these challenges. I include a few examples of practical relationship building exercises, which colleagues are using successfully, and further examples of relational teaching and co-creation can be found in Chapters 3 and 4.

Example 2.1

The 'collective challenge' by Timothee Parrique, Stockholm University, Sweden

In the 'collective challenge' the teacher uses PowerPoint and electronic voting devices in a large group to present students with multiple choice questions. They have a limited amount of time to answer the questions. To complete the challenge the whole class needs to reach a certain percentage of correct answers, for example, more than 75 per cent of individual answers need to be correct. Discussion and collaboration is encouraged but books, notes and digital devices are not allowed. The questions are designed specifically to require higher-order thinking and need students to collaborate. The process is followed by group reflection on the process (Barrineau et al, 2019).

Example 2.2

'Two stage examinations' (Levy et al, 2018; Weiman et al, 2014)

'Two stage examinations' offer another clever way of involving students in collaborating in large groups. This initiative, which has been practised in physics education, consists of a first stage involving a typical individual exam or class test, followed by a second stage where students are actively encouraged to work in groups to do another test, usually answering the same questions or a subset of questions from the first test. Students tend to achieve better grades in and enjoy, the second half of the exam due to the collaboration between students that frequently leads to greater group overall knowledge (Levy et al, 2018; Weiman et al, 2014).

Example 2.3

'Parlor talk' by Werder et al (2010) at Western Washington University, USA

Werder et al (2010, p 28) describe how some students reported that they did not feel connected with some of their teachers despite wanting to connect.

They said that by knowing things about me – things I initially saw as trivial, like what music I listened to – they were better able to relate to me. And as a result of this connection they wanted to do the work. Being so focused on covering my lessons in the previous weeks, I had missed this simple formula: Pay attention to who my students are as people, and they will pay more attention to me and their learning. Allow all of us to share who we are outside the classroom and we can connect better inside, making for a better learning experience – for all of us.

Summary

- Positive teacher–student and student–student relationships in learning and teaching are powerful predictors of enhanced student outcomes, and yet relationship building is not prioritised due to concerns about maintaining professional distance, lack of professional development to support relational teaching, large classes and poor use of existing evidence to inform teaching approaches.

- Relational pedagogy is perhaps a more established concept within school education, but can easily translate into relational approaches to teaching in HE.

- In UK HE, interest is growing in the role of relationships, belonging and emotions as ways of achieving positive student outcomes.

- Time spent building trust and relationships is time well spent, because relationships form the foundation of good teaching.

Useful texts

Felten, P and Lambert, L M (2020) *Relationship-Rich Education: How Human Connections Drive Success in College*. Baltimore, MD: Johns Hopkins University Press.

An overview of the importance of relationships across HE campuses. The book contains many authentic examples from across US universities and colleges.

Finkel, D L (2000) *Teaching with Your Mouth Shut*. Portsmouth: Heinemann.

A critique of the transmission model of teaching with a range of alternatives. Contains some highly nuanced stories and accounts of teaching approaches.

Quinlan, K M (2016) How Emotion Matters in Four Key Relationships in Teaching and Learning in Higher Education. *College Teaching*, 64: 101–11.

Quinlan argues that emotion has been overlooked in HE literature. She redresses this by arguing for the importance of four key relationships: students' relationship with the subject; with the teacher; with their peers; and with themselves.

What they were advocating was not a longer list of topics to choose from; rather they were arguing for a move away from curriculum as delivery to curriculum as the joint making of meaning.

(Fielding, 2001, pp 127–8)

Introduction to related concepts

Lubicz-Nawrocka (2020), in her PhD research, found that all the students she interviewed from different universities in Scotland, without exception, said the courses where they had the opportunity to co-create with a teacher were the best courses they experienced at university. This research outcome and other benefits we are seeing increasingly demonstrated in research literature suggests that we need to pay more attention to co-creation in the classroom. In this chapter, I introduce what co-creation is, and then offer an overview of the benefits and challenges, as well as some examples of co-creating learning and teaching. Co-creation is closely related to, and overlaps with, a number of other terms, which I briefly outline here.

Student engagement

Defining student engagement is a contentious issue in HE (Bryson, 2014; Wolf-Wendell et al, 2009). In a commonly cited definition, Kuh et al (2005, p 9) argue that student engagement is comprised of two parts:

the first is the amount of time and effort students put into their studies and other activities that lead to the experiences and outcomes that constitute student success. The second is the ways the institution allocates resources and organizes learning opportunities and services to induce students to participate in and benefit from such activities.

Bryson (2014, p 18) helpfully describes these two elements of student engagement as '*students engaging*' (what the student does) and '*engaging students*' (what the institution does).

Buckley (2014) highlights the differences between student engagement in governance (student representation on university committees, and other quality assurance and enhancement activities) and student engagement in pedagogy (engagement in learning, teaching, assessment and curriculum enhancement). It is also important to acknowledge that students are not simply engaged or not, but rather, engagement has what Cuba et al (2016, p 144) describe as a *'particularistic nature'*. They argue that students in different contexts experience *'episodic'*, *'sustained'*, or *'cumulative'* engagement (p 149). The danger of a broad conceptualisation of student engagement is that the term is used to refer to anything from a student turning up to class through to a student who is highly motivated and goes beyond course requirements (as well as very different levels of institutional activity to engage students).

Active learning

Active learning aims to involve students in the learning process and often refers to activities such as writing, discussion, small group work, as well as values and attitude exploration (Bonwell and Eison, 1981; Freeman et al, 2014; Michael, 2006). Michael (2016, p 162) argues that *'meaningful learning is facilitated by articulating explanations, whether to one's self, peers, or teachers'*. These ways of learning are impossible without interaction between teacher and students, and between students and students. Mayhew et al (2016, p 550) add that:

seemingly irrefutable evidence demonstrates that active and engaged learning practices yield substantial benefits over traditional lecture based formats in which students passively receive information. These outcomes include greater verbal and quantitative skills, subject matter competence, cognitive and intellectual skills, openness to diversity, intercultural competence, leadership, citizenship, and moral development.

Critical issues

Are we negligent for not implementing active learning?

Freeman et al (2014) synthesise research on active learning in science, technology, engineering and mathematics, outlining substantial benefits for students in terms of enhanced academic performance. They argue that if the research results they demonstrated for the positive benefits of active learning had been found in a randomised control trial for a medical treatment, the control condition (lectures with little or no interaction) would be discontinued. I suggest therefore that Freeman et al's work points to our continued negligence in HE for withholding an educational approach from students that has been proven to be effective. Importantly, many of the studies the authors examined only involved active learning for 10–15 per cent of the lecture time, but were still able to demonstrate positive outcomes.

High rates of student enrolment at university are not always matched by increasing numbers of teachers. What results in many cases is larger classes. However, large classes usually have a detrimental effect on levels of active learning, interaction, student engagement and student learning (Cuseo, 2007; Gibbs, 2012). Gibbs (2010) notes that dialogue in larger classes tends to focus on fact clarification rather than on exploration of concepts. While smaller classes may be more conducive to interaction, we must beware of assuming that active learning will magically happen in a smaller class, or that it is not possible to learn actively in a larger class. The teacher has a key role to play: '*active learning doesn't just happen; it occurs in the classroom when the teacher creates a learning environment that makes it more likely to occur*' (Michael, 2016, p 164).

Critical issues

How large is a large class?

Someone once related to me their experiences of being a student in a class of over 1000 students – that is a big class. Classes of 300–500 students are relatively common in universities in the UK, and there is no doubt that these are also large classes. However 50 to 100 students can feel like a large class if you normally teach a class of 40 students. A colleague from music education suggested to me that anything over four or five students in his subject can be considered a large class because of the style of teaching he expects to use. Context is clearly important. It is very hard to say definitively when a class changes from a small class to a medium class to a large class. Is it when students do not fit in the room comfortably or when it becomes impossible to learn students' names? In online settings, a class can feel big once it becomes difficult to moderate whole group or multiple small group discussions without requiring teaching assistants to help with this moderation.

Cuseo (2007), drawing on existing research, proposed an ideal class size of 15. Cuseo (2007, p 15) argues '*this could be accomplished without incurring added institutional cost by increasing the size of some existing large-sized classes, which is not likely to have adverse effects on student learning because their existing size already puts them well beyond the point of optimal returns*'. Victoria University, Melbourne, has invested in making first-year classes smaller, and I outline this example further in Chapter 5.

Students are sometimes resistant to becoming actively engaged in class, possibly because students get used to teaching that does not require them to interact, and these habits can be hard to break. When teachers communicate early in students' university experience their expectations that learning and teaching at university are active processes, as well as outlining some of the benefits of interaction, it can be easier to encourage students to interact.

Student–staff partnership in learning and teaching

In the last five years we have seen new journals, books and significant activity in HE under the banner of student–staff partnership or *students as partners*. One commonly cited definition of student–staff partnership is '*a collaborative, reciprocal process through which all participants have the opportunity to contribute equally, although not necessarily in the same ways, to curricular or pedagogical conceptualization, decision-making, implementation, investigation, or analysis*' (Cook-Sather et al, 2014, pp 6–7). In this definition, partnership implies a level of equality between students and teachers, but this can sometimes seem challenging; for example, where teachers grade students' work, or where staff decide which students to invite to become partners or make other early decisions before students are involved (Bovill, 2014 and 2018; Heron, 1992).

However, it is possible for students to be involved in decision-making about their learning from an early stage through, for example, curriculum planning groups that include students who will be studying the course in the future (Mihans et al, 2008). Many partnership initiatives involve a few students, selected to work with staff on research and Scholarship of Teaching and Learning (SoTL) projects or university enhancement projects (Mercer-Mapstone et al, 2017; Mercer-Mapstone and Bovill, 2019; Sims et al, 2016). There are also schemes where students observe teaching and then have feedback discussions with a teacher about ways to enhance learning and teaching (Cook-Sather, 2010; Huxham et al, 2017; Scoles et al, 2019). These project-based selective partnerships differ from examples where teachers engage the whole class of students to negotiate learning and teaching (Bovill, 2019b; Bryson et al, 2015; Moore-Cherry et al, 2015).

Critical issues

Two participation models

Students and staff might not reach full partnership in all aspects of the design of a course. It can help to recognise that there might be stages in

→

a course when it is more appropriate for staff to lead, and other stages or aspects of learning and teaching where it is more appropriate for students to lead. I present two frameworks that can help us to envision these nuances in the nature of student participation.

1. The Ladder of student participation in curriculum design

Based on Sherry Arnstein's (1969) model of citizen participation, the *Ladder of student participation in curriculum design* illustrates different types of student participation (Figure 3.1). Note that partnership is relatively high up the ladder. The original article by Bovill and Bulley (2011) offers further discussion and critique.

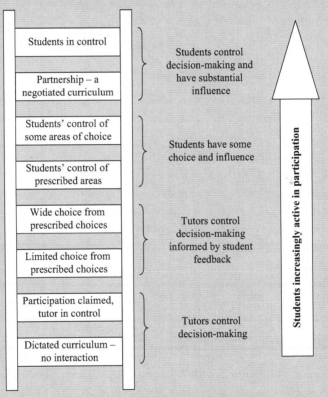

Figure 3.1 The Ladder of student participation in curriculum design (Bovill and Bulley, 2011). Reprinted with kind permission of Oxford Brookes University.

29

2. The participation matrix

A participation matrix is a framework which enables transparency about how different participants or stakeholders participate at different stages of a collaboration. Each stage of an initiative can be mapped against these levels of participation.

The participation matrix is based on the premise that it might not be desirable to aim for full partnership all the time and that students or staff may be in control at different stages of work... Ideally, teachers and students come together to plan and undertake work, but where one person starts a project and then encourages other colleagues to join, the matrix can be helpful in highlighting who of those involved need to lead, work in partnership, participate, be consulted, or simply be informed about specific elements of work and when.

(Bovill, 2017a, p 4)

Co-creating learning and teaching

In conversations I have had with teachers, they can sometimes be reluctant to use the term partnership because they fear it sounds too radical. In other situations, people use partnership and co-creation interchangeably or see co-creation as a form of partnership. Bovill et al (2016, p 196) describe co-creation as occurring *'when staff and students work collaboratively with one another to create components of curricula and/or pedagogical approaches'*. Interestingly, Fielding (1999) and Scoles (2019) argue that collegiality may be a more appropriate term than collaborative, because *'despite its collective surface, collaboration remains a form of individualism because it is, or could be, rooted in self-interest: collaboration is, in effect, a plural form of individualism'* (Fielding, 1999, p 6). In contrast, collegiality *'involves a mutually positive attitude between fellow professionals; it is necessarily reciprocal and as such cannot be sustained by only one of the parties involved'* (Fielding, 1999, p 14).

In my own work (Bovill, 2019b), I argue that co-creation differs from active learning in the expectation that students will share decision-making and adopt increased agency within the co-creation process. Lubicz-Nawrocka (2020, p xii) captures this sense of shared decision-making within her definition of co-creation of the curriculum, as *'the values-based implementation of an ongoing, reciprocal, creative, and mutually beneficial process of staff and students working together to negotiate and share decision-making regarding aspects of higher education curricula'*. Moreover, Iversen and Stavnskaer Pedersen (2017, p 22) argue that *'in co-creation both the "co" and the "creation" are significant. The "co" signals that the process is social and the "creation", that something new appears as a consequence of the process'.*

Co-creation and partnership share many values and characteristics, and both envisage learning and teaching as things done *with* students not done *to* students (Bovill et al, 2011; Shor, 1992). Co-creation and partnership both emphasise:

» shared goals;

» shared decision-making;

» negotiation;

» valuing student perspectives;

» shared respect;

» shared responsibility;

» reciprocity.

The main difference between partnership and co-creation, I argue, is the level of equality often implied by partnership.

Personally, I see the terms student engagement, active learning, partnership and co-creation as roughly an overlapping continuum of student participation, where the level of meaningful participation, shared decision-making, shared responsibility and equality increases as you move from student engagement to partnership (see Figure 3.2).

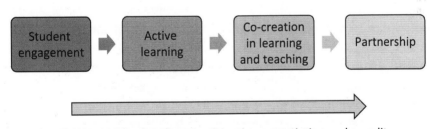

Increasing levels of student participation, negotiation and equality

Figure 3.2 A simplified continuum of common participation terminology.

Sometimes people might claim to be working in partnership, but if individual experiences of partnership fall short of equality, it can result in making students and staff cynical about future partnership. Indeed, the language and behaviour of those claiming partnership can sometimes be at odds with their enacted practice (Bovill,

2015 and 2017b; Cook-Sather et al, 2014). I once facilitated a partnership workshop where a senior staff member told the student member of their group to order a taxi. Her behaviour could be interpreted in different ways, but the student was spoken to dismissively and treated in this instance as a helper, not a partner.

Another way in which you often see the gap between the rhetoric and enacted practice of partnership is in joint conference presentations given by staff and students (Bovill, 2017b; Wilson et al, 2020). Some presentations are given in ways that enact genuine partnership, but other presentations do not include student presenters' names in the conference programme, are led or dominated by staff, involve staff speaking over students or on behalf of students, and involve giving students a small or unimportant role. Staff also often take over answering questions from the audience; sometimes explained by the questions student presenters receive. Indeed, Wilson et al (2020) describe female student presenters being challenged inappropriately by audience members about their manner of presentation in a way staff or male students would be unlikely to be challenged. Yet when staff answer on students' behalf, this can signal a lack of trust or a fear of letting go by staff, and demonstrates behaviour inconsistent with partnership. Those working on partnership projects involving only a small number of students may find it easier to select students (or invite all students involved) to present at a conference. When working with a whole class, it is less obvious which students should be invited to give a conference presentation. All too often the most engaged, able and eloquent students are chosen, or those who have the closest relationship to the teacher.

A common misunderstanding of co-creation is that the teacher's subject expertise is no longer important; on the contrary, teachers' expertise is still key, but alongside this expertise, teachers may need to develop a range of facilitation, guidance and co-inquiry skills, and the ability to ask challenging questions (Breen and Littlejohn, 2000; Cook-Sather et al, 2014; Otis and Hammond, 2010; Thayer-Bacon, 2010). Finkel (2000) also highlights that power over the classroom can be shared with students but the teacher still has a role and ultimately retains authority. Importantly, co-creation of learning and teaching does not remove the students' need to learn knowledge, skills and ways of practising in a discipline. As Werder et al (2010, p 30) argue, in thinking about students, 'we must first believe that they really are essential to the conversation'. A value is placed on student perspectives and capabilities in a way that is often absent in mainstream teaching. Students' ideas and perspectives can enhance learning and teaching and contribute to knowledge co-construction in ways that staff cannot necessarily predict.

I provide some examples to help illustrate a variety of co-creation practices involving a whole class of students.

Example 3.1

Co-creating the 'Entrepreneurship and Business Planning' course at the University of St Andrews, Scotland, UK – Ignacio Canales

In this course, Professor Canales invited 50 third- and fourth-year students to design group projects to create a business idea. The whole class then co-created the course by identifying what they needed to learn in order to be able to successfully complete the students' proposed group projects. Students then identified and read articles and resources relevant to the projects before presenting important ideas from these materials to their peers in class using engaging and entertaining teaching approaches (Bovill, 2019b; Cook-Sather et al, 2014).

Example 3.2

Co-creating a statistics course at Elon University, North Carolina, USA – Ayesha Delpish

In this first-year statistics course, Dr Delpish worked with 33 students to co-create and negotiate what took place in each class.

By opening negotiations with the students from the 1st day of the course, I was able to create an environment where power could be genuinely shared. For example, any question raised by a student during class went back to the entire group with a simple What do you think and why? All stakeholders made every class-level decision after discussing different possibilities.

(Delpish et al, 2010, p 108)

Example 3.3

Co-creating the 'Understanding Gender in the Contemporary World' course at the University of Edinburgh, Scotland, UK – Meryl Kenny

Dr Kenny worked with 12 students on a course entitled 'Social and Political Science in Practice'. During this course, third- and fourth-year students

$\longrightarrow$

worked in partnership with Dr Kenny to research and co-create a new course: 'Understanding Gender in the Contemporary World'. The students identified key topics and concepts for the course, and developed and piloted learning resources and activities. The understanding gender course was then offered to first- and second-year students within the university course catalogue the following year (Kenny, 2019).

Example 3.4

Co-creating a course evaluation at Queen Margaret University, Edinburgh, Scotland, UK – Catherine Bovill

In this postgraduate course, I invited 21 students to co-create the course evaluation with me. Students were studying an 'Introduction to Educational Research' course and had been learning about evaluation research. The students were invited to volunteer on their own or in pairs or groups to lead evaluations of different aspects of the course using whichever methods of data collection they wanted to use. The students collaborated with me to collate, analyse and disseminate the results of the evaluation (Bovill et al, 2010).

Example 3.5

Co-creating essay titles within a classics course at Reading University, England, UK and at the University of Vienna, Austria – Peter Kruschwitz

In a classics course at Reading University, Professor Kruschwitz invited approximately 80 students to design their own essay titles after he gave them six to eight keywords. The students then submitted their draft titles to him so he could guide them if they designed a question that was too narrow or broad in scope. Over the years he has used this approach with hundreds of students. His evaluations demonstrate that students have increased interest and motivation for this assessment and enhanced performance (Cook-Sather et al, 2014). He has also introduced a similar approach in his more recent teaching at the University of Vienna, Austria.

Example 3.6

Shared negotiation of assessment weighting in an engineering course at the University of Glasgow, Scotland, UK – Donald Ballance

Dr Ballance invites 400 students on his first-year engineering skills course at the University of Glasgow to decide the weightings of each of the four assignments that are required for the communications part of the course: a group report; a group presentation; a group poster; and an individual report involving peer review. The students vote for the weighting they would rather have for each of these assignments. Even if a student votes for 100 per cent individual report, it is explained that all four assessments will take place, but they can influence the relative emphasis placed on each assessment. The weightings are then adjusted (and tend to vary from year to year depending on students' preferences), and the assessment weightings are the same for all students. Even though students may not end up with the outcome they would personally prefer, most students appreciate that they have had the opportunity to influence this element of their course.

What is noticeable from these examples is that most of them take place in smaller classes of approximately 50 or less. The engineering example is a much bigger class, but perhaps what is being described is enabling students to be consulted and have choice, rather than more in-depth shared decision-making and negotiation. We will return to this issue of whether it is possible to undertake whole class co-creation with larger groups of students in Chapter 5.

Benefits of co-creating learning and teaching

There are many benefits to students and staff from the processes and outcomes of co-creation. Cook-Sather et al (2014) highlight three broad positive outcomes from co-creation and partnership which are shared by students and staff, even if they are experienced in slightly different ways. First, co-creation of learning and teaching leads to increased engagement, in the form of enhanced motivation and greater learning. Second, we see enhanced awareness, as students gain a greater meta-cognitive awareness of how they and their peers learn, helping them develop a stronger sense of identity. Staff also report a greater awareness of why they make particular choices in their teaching and the impact of those choices. Third, there is evidence of enhancement of learning and teaching, with students and staff reporting improved teaching and learning experiences. In a systematic literature review of partnership practices in HE, Mercer-Mapstone et al (2017) report some related benefits in terms of greater student academic performance, students having an enhanced sense of belonging, increased confidence, and enhanced relationships and trust.

Much of the evidence of benefits from partnership and co-creation has not specifically distinguished between outcomes from co-creation with a whole group of students and teacher in the classroom, and co-creation and partnership projects involving just a few students (even if these partnership projects are taking place university-wide). Within my own work (Bovill, 2019b), I have highlighted the specific findings from whole-class co-creation of learning and teaching. The following summary is adapted from this work. Drawing on the work of Bergmark and Westman (2016); Bovill (2014); Bovill et al (2010); Deeley (2014); Deeley and Bovill (2017); and Delpish et al (2010), I note that the benefits and broader outcomes for students include:

> » improved academic performance and higher quality of work;
> » enhanced skills for future professional development including teamwork, critical reflection and communication skills;
> » learning beyond the course and transferring learning into new contexts;
> » greater academic aspirations;
> » opening up the learning process to be more transparent;
> » a fun process;
> » shift from a focus on grades to learning;
> » increased confidence, enthusiasm, engagement and motivation;
> » increased autonomy, self-regulation and responsibility;
> » increased ownership;
> » students appreciating learning by doing and learning collaboratively with other students;
> » students appreciating being asked to voice opinions;
> » practice at working democratically;
> » students feeling valued;
> » students developing and experiencing a more equal relationship with the teacher;
> » lack of familiarity and shock at being asked to co-create a course.

In addition, the previous list of authors, along with Huxham et al (2015), report outcomes that are experienced by both students and staff in the form of:

» enhanced identity, meta-cognitive awareness of learning and teaching;

» feeling personally inspired and/or transformed;

» creation of a learning community;

» enhanced negotiation experience and skills;

» curriculum becoming more (socially) relevant;

» student and teacher roles change.

Finally, according to Bergmark and Westman (2016); Bovill (2014); Delpish et al (2010); and Huxham et al (2015), academic staff also report that whole-class co-creation:

» is risky and unpredictable;

» poses challenges in getting the pace of teaching right;

» but is also transformative.

Co-creation seems to make learning and teaching processes more transparent for everyone. As Otis and Hammond (2010, p 40) observe, '*students often remark that they never realized how much their professors care about their teaching, and, conversely, faculty frequently comment that they never realized how deeply students care about their learning*'. Barrineau et al (2019) report colleagues' experiences of active student participation (ASP) and co-creation: Sanna Barrineau describes '*realising quickly how cheated I had felt throughout my own inactive and non-participatory studies at university*' (p 8), Alexis Engström talks about having experiences which '*left me with a hard-to-cure curiosity about further collaborations around the topic of learning*' (p 9), while Guy Finkill argues that: '*to experience any other form of education now would feel like nothing less than a fundamental step into the past*' (p 58).

Challenges of co-creating learning and teaching

Although a positive picture is emerging of the benefits of co-creation, there are many challenges (Bovill et al, 2016; Cook-Sather et al, 2014). We have already mentioned the added difficulty of co-creating learning and teaching in large classes, and the problems that arise when people claim to be sharing decision-making, but in reality they maintain authority.

Bovill et al (2016) highlight three key challenges of co-creation. The first challenge is overcoming resistance to co-creation. Some staff and students may have genuine and well-founded concerns about changing their approach to teaching and learning. For example a student who is used to getting A grades in her assessed work may be nervous about the introduction of a new co-created assessment. Staff may have concerns about handing over power to students when they wish to cover substantial content and they are unconvinced that students know enough about the subject to be co-creating classes. Any reluctance on the part of students can often be reduced if clear ideas, plans and goals for co-creation are shared with students. If staff are encouraged to consider a range of different elements of learning and teaching that might be co-created – not just specialist content knowledge but, for example, which case studies might be of more interest, or how a group work exercise might proceed – they are often more willing to see that student perspectives could be valuable.

Critical questions for practice

Reflection on the co-creation in your teaching

» Do you feel there are some areas of your teaching which are more or less appropriate for students to co-create?

» Why?

Consider sharing, with one of your colleagues (staff or student), your views about which areas of your teaching are more or less appropriate to co-create.

» What are your colleague's views?

» How do they compare to your views?

The second challenge highlighted by Bovill et al (2016) is navigating institutional structures, practices and norms. Many universities are set up in ways that envisage teaching as something done to students and in which students play a minimal role. University systems for course design and approval typically take a long time and some teachers interpret these structures as closing down possibilities for co-creation, but there are examples of staff and students finding ways to work within these constraints as well as lobbying to change them. One example from my own practice when I worked at the University of Glasgow was that I invited students on a Masters in Learning and

Teaching in HE programme to co-design one of their dissertation learning outcomes. Although a set of learning outcomes were created for the dissertation by me, I included in the official paperwork the statement '*plus one additional learning outcome designed by the student in collaboration with their supervisor*'. The students were assessed against all the learning outcomes including their own. The course approval process went relatively smoothly due to providing a clear but flexible plan for learning.

The third challenge highlighted by Bovill et al (2016) was establishing an inclusive co-creation approach. Ensuring inclusivity in co-creation and partnership is a growing area of concern (Bovill, 2019b; Cook-Sather, 2018 and 2019; Marquis et al, 2018; Mercer-Mapstone and Bovill, 2019; Mercer-Mapstone et al, 2019). Some of the selective partnership projects, common to institutions in the UK, may be simply engaging already engaged students, and in some instances are exacerbating already existing structural inequalities. I have argued that whole-class approaches to co-creation might solve some of these exclusion concerns by removing the need to select students (Bovill, 2019b; Mercer-Mapstone and Bovill, 2019). However, even in cases where a whole group is invited to co-create learning and teaching, care needs to be taken to ensure genuine engagement is possible in a range of different ways and at different times by all students, but particularly traditionally underserved students.

Critical question for practice

Reflection on diversity and inclusion within your teaching

Look at the following online resources:

Increasing inclusivity in the classroom: https://cft.vanderbilt.edu/guides-sub-pages/increasing-inclusivity-in-the-classroom/ (Greer, nd).

Expanding the conversation: Developing inclusive pedagogy modules: http://queensu.ca/equity/EDIonline (Queen's University, nd).

» How do you, or can you, ensure that under-represented students or those who face structural inequalities are engaged in your classes?

Another perceived challenge to co-creation has been the constraints that teachers experience from working in subjects where there is a professional body. Professional bodies often set particular knowledge and competencies required of a graduate, but commonly do not dictate how the subject is taught in order to develop these outcomes

(Cook-Sather et al, 2014). This provides a degree of flexibility for co-creation within an accredited programme.

Setting out to design and enact teaching and learning as a shared endeavour can feel risky to staff (Bovill, 2014). Staff often have concerns about facing a wall of silence from students if they pose questions or suggest handing over some responsibility for learning and teaching. Students can often think that it is the teacher's job to teach, and universities can create the impression in the first few weeks that the student's job is simply to sit, listen and take notes if all they offer is teaching delivery. However:

to engage in learning always entails the risk that learning might have an impact on you, that learning might change you. This means that education only begins when the learner is willing to take a risk. One way of putting this is to say that one of the constituents of the educational relationship is trust. Why are risk and trust related? This is fundamentally because trust is about those situations in which you do not know and cannot know what can happen... to suggest that education can be and should be risk free... is a misrepresentation of what education is about.

(Biesta, 2006, pp 25–6)

Yet, with good planning, and if staff are willing to share their rationale for why they want to negotiate teaching and learning, and with many opportunities to ask questions, it is amazing how quickly staff and students can start to see new ways to relate to one another and to transform classrooms.

Finally, one other important challenge that must be mentioned is that of time. In Chapter 2, I highlighted that lack of time can be a challenge for teachers and students in building relationships – similarly, lack of time can be a barrier for co-creating learning and teaching. Most students and staff are time pressured, and co-creation can require more space in class to enable shared negotiation processes to take place. And yet in my experience it is not the staff or students who have lots of spare time who engage with co-creation; it usually involves a change of priorities. The first time that this approach is taken it might take more planning time – most classes take more time to plan the first time you teach them – but because whole-class co-creation is focused on learning and teaching during scheduled class time, it requires a change to the way we do education rather than necessarily a change to the amount of time we spend on it. This said, when students and staff find learning and teaching more rewarding, they often invest more time in teaching.

Towards personal transformation through transformation of learning and teaching

When teachers co-create learning and teaching, they frequently report that it has been a transformational experience. After adopting a co-creation approach, one teacher stated: *It was liberating... we moved from teaching... that just didn't work to... [teaching]... that... was put together in ways that I never even imagined were possible... so... it's really transformed how I think about teaching and how I teach.* (Bovill, 2014, p 18) And as Iversen and Stavnskaer Pedersen (2017, p 23) report, *'Being with students changes me'.* One student describes his experiences of negotiating learning with his teacher:

the more I thought about it, the more it shook up everything I associated with education and learning; how I had done homework, written papers – everything has been completely turned on end. I had been watching my education pass me by without ever taking part... I finally understood why partnerships in teaching and learning are so crucial. To be able to learn from my professors I had to be mature enough to want something besides grades and a diploma from my education.

(Manor et al, 2010, pp 5–6)

Ultimately, positive relationships between teachers and students, and between students and students, change the way we think about one another, the conversations we have, and transform our understanding of learning and teaching.

Summary

- Student engagement, active learning, partnership and co-creating learning and teaching all lead to improved student outcomes. They can be conceptualised as a continuum from student engagement to partnership with increasing levels of shared decision-making and equality associated with partnership.

- Co-creating learning and teaching assumes that students have valuable contributions to make to teaching and learning.

- Co-creating learning and teaching changes the teaching approach to something done *with* students rather than something done *to* students.

- Examples of co-created learning and teaching tend to be found more frequently in classes with 50 students or less. Co-creation is possible with larger

$\longrightarrow$

41

classes, but might involve enhanced choice and active learning rather than deeper forms of highly negotiated co-creation.

- Many students and staff find co-creation to be risky and challenging, but it can also be transformative.

Useful texts

Barrineau, S, Engström, A and Schnaas, U (2019) *An Active Student Participation Companion*. Uppsala: Uppsala University. [online] Available at: www.diva-portal. org/smash/get/diva2:1286438/FULLTEXT02.pdf (accessed 12 January 2020).

An overview of co-creation of learning and teaching, although the book uses the term 'active student participation'. Informed by the work of the Centre for Environment and Development Studies (CEMUS) at Uppsala University in Sweden, this book provides relevant literature and foundational ideas, useable models and examples of active student participation.

Bovill, C (2019a) A Co-Creation of Learning and Teaching Typology: What Kind of Co-Creation are you Planning or Doing? *International Journal for Students as Partners*, 3. [online] Available at: https://mulpress.mcmaster.ca/ijsap/article/view/3953 (accessed 12 January 2020).

This article outlines different types of co-creation that are possible, highlighting variation in, for example, the number of students involved, the focus of co-creation and whether students are rewarded or not for their contributions.

Bovill, C and Woolmer, C (2019) How Conceptualisations of Curriculum in Higher Education Influence Student-Staff Co-Creation *in* and *of* the Curriculum. *Higher Education*, 78: 407–22.

Offering an overview of how curriculum definitions influence what students are invited to co-create, this article also outlines a distinction between co-creation in *and* of *the curriculum.*

Chapter 4 | Towards relational pedagogy in higher education

Good teaching is an act of hospitality.

(Palmer, 1998, p 50)

Introduction

We have seen in the previous chapters that there are many benefits from relational teaching and co-creating learning and teaching, but these concepts are often not brought together despite them being closely connected. Relational pedagogy and co-creating learning and teaching build meaningful relationships based on values of trust, shared respect and the importance of dialogue. In this chapter, I will argue that these approaches can be mutually reinforcing. Building good relationships creates a foundation for co-creating learning and teaching, but in turn co-creation of learning and teaching can strengthen positive relationships between teacher and students, and between students and students. I also explore the importance of teachers maximising the opportunities they have to develop deeper collegial relationships with students, and I offer some practical suggestions of how this might be done.

Relationships are a foundation for co-creation

All too often in HE, teaching takes place in ways in which staff and students remain anonymous to one another. In large classes, a teacher is unlikely to know all the students. Anonymous marking also often forms a barrier to relationship building between student and teacher focused on assessment (Pitt and Winstone, 2018). Students regularly experience inconsistencies of provision, where *some teachers care deeply and some not at all'* (Baik et al, 2019, p 7). As Chris Manor, a student at Elon University, North Carolina states:

to this day Stephen… is the only teacher who has asked me what I wanted to get out of taking class. Ever. I had never even thought about it? What I want to get out of a class, how does class relate to me? I grew up thinking what I assumed every other student thought and the majority of students still think – what do I want to get out of class? An A. The thought of actively trying to learn something never crossed my mind.

(Manor et al, 2010, p 5)

This is a stark reminder that many students are drifting through university with little engagement (Arum and Roksa, 2011). So how do we establish environments conducive to relationship building? Several key ideas are explored in the next few sections.

The first five minutes and beyond

We set the tone in our first conversations with students. Plevin (2017, p 67) argues that '*outside your classroom before the lesson is a great opportunity to get talking to your students*'. Try to break the ice by asking something about their weekend or comment on something in the news or on social media. Try to learn students' names (Felten and Lambert, 2020; Thomas, 2012). This can help you to forge the first connections before you have entered the classroom with a new class. All too often expectations are influenced by the unwritten rules about how students and teachers should behave; as Shor (1992, p 2) describes, his students '*were waiting for the teacher to arrive and do education to them*'.

We have the power to transform classroom experiences, and '*early teacher-student and student-student encounters are crucial in relationship building*' (Bovill, 2019b, p 9). Gozemba (2002a, p 132) reports a student saying to her: '*When you come to class on the first day and the teacher says "We notice your attitude," they forget that we notice their attitude too. Students do the same thing*'. It may be a bit of a cliché that first impressions last, but for relationship building, teachers can consciously take steps to build better relationships right from the first encounter with a new group of students. The first five minutes is an amazing opportunity to set the tone for the kind of classroom you wish to build. Teachers need to demonstrate that they have a desire to get to know students, that they value contributions from students and that they are prepared to give something of themselves. How a teacher responds to a student's first contribution to class can signal very clearly to students whether their contributions are welcome or not. While time is needed to build trust and respect with any new group of people, the first five minutes, and the rest of the first class, can make it easier or harder for a teacher and students to build relationships over the coming weeks and months. Trust and respect are fundamental underpinnings for co-creation (as well as outcomes of co-creation), but they need to be established from the outset and given time to develop fully. Take time to explain why you plan to co-create, outlining how co-creation might take place and the variety of roles everyone might adopt – setting out clear intentions and different options can make it more inviting and easier for all students to engage. Provide plenty of opportunities for discussion and questions.

Example 4.1

Building hospitality for students online, MSc Clinical Education, University of Edinburgh, Scotland, UK – Gill Aitken, Tim Fawns, Derek Jones, Janette Jamieson and Debbie Spence

The online MSc in Clinical Education programme at the University of Edinburgh has witnessed strong growth in student numbers over recent years. In 2019–20, 207 students were enrolled across the three years of the programme. The whole team of academic and professional services staff work closely together to aspire to an ethic of hospitality throughout, but particularly in the first two to three weeks. They pay attention to the contexts in which students will be teaching and learning, remaining open to adapting course design in response as needed. Rather than asking students to give up their cultures and practices, the team instead makes space for students to shape the learning environment through their background, culture, perspective and experience. Although the team prioritises hospitality, they emphasise that they *don't own the house*; the online spaces are perceived as shared and co-constructed spaces. In practical terms they have found that the significant time invested in building positive relationships and emphasising hospitality in the early weeks of the programme pays off. For example, on the odd occasion there is a technical hitch, students have been more forgiving – perhaps offering more understanding because they have built a human relationship with the teachers facing the challenge.

We are aware of many cases in our programme... where face-to-face interactions are absent, yet there are still strong and trusting student-teacher relationships. We have developed practices over time that make use of our technologies and their accumulation of digital traces (email trails, online discussion postings, printed lists of student names, photos, occupations, locations, websites and search engines), to support social presence, communication and understanding of our students.

(Fawns et al, 2019, p 2)

However, it is also important to recognise that all of this takes time and this approach is not easily scalable, without investment of adequate resources.

Getting to know one another and enhancing the relevance of education

We need to be mindful of continuing the process of getting to know students throughout their time at university; indeed, Felten and Lambert (2020) talk about the importance of students experiencing *relentless welcome*. By making efforts to get to know the interests of students, we can also respond in ways to ensure that teaching becomes more relevant for students. Rogers and Freiberg (1994, p 35) claimed that:

nearly every student finds that large portions of the curriculum are meaningless. Thus education becomes the futile attempt to learn material that has no personal meaning. Such learning involves the mind only: it is learning that takes place 'from the neck up'. It does not involve feelings or personal meanings; it has no relevance for the whole person.

Shor (1992) describes teaching a class where he was just not connecting to the students and felt he wasn't getting anywhere. Instead of ploughing on and having a tough class for the semester, he paused and asked students what the problem was. Eventually, one student spoke up and explained how upset and annoyed he and some of the other students were with the class test they had completed prior to class, which they considered unfair. By taking time to ask questions and find out what was concerning students, Shor gradually found that the students opened up. Working together, the class devised a range of better approaches and solutions to the test, which they proposed to the College. This approach enabled respect and trust to grow between Shor and the students so they could progress towards more meaningful experiences over the rest of the semester. Shor moved from trying to implement a pre-determined plan for teaching towards shared decision-making with students about the direction of their learning.

Dialogue and active listening

One way of getting to know students better and building relationships is to ensure that there is regular dialogue between staff and students: *'relationships are built on dialogue and it's a lot easier to strike up a conversation with a student if you can talk about something which actually interests them'* (Plevin, 2017, p 81). This is not just idle conversation:

dialogue is open-ended; that is, in a genuine dialogue neither party knows at the outset what the outcome or decision will be... dialogue is a common search for understanding, empathy, or appreciation. It can be playful or serious, logical or imaginative, goal or process oriented, but it is always a genuine quest for something undetermined at the beginning.

(Noddings, 1992, p 23)

Noddings continues:

part of what is learned in dialogue is interpersonal reasoning – the capacity to communicate, share decision making, arrive at compromises and support each other in solving everyday problems.

(p 53)

A teacher can listen to what a student says and learn about them, but when a teacher actively listens, the student's ideas and emotions become something that influences the teacher in how they respond, and in how and what they teach. McDaniel (2010, p 100) argues that the process of dialogue helps us to gain '*a deeper sense of how the world seems to others*' and this enables us to realise that there is more of the world beyond ourselves.

Responsive teaching involves a teacher adapting what and how they are teaching in direct response to listening to students' ideas, interests and needs. In some classes, teachers also spend time teaching students to actively listen to one another. As Werder et al (2010, p 17) argue, '*while discussion has a primary goal of convergence (reaching the best solution or answer), dialogue has a primary goal of divergence – exchanging a broad range of perspectives to achieve a deeper understanding*'. Focusing on more responsive teaching and divergent assessments can be a powerful way of ensuring that the teacher is not seen as the conduit to all ideas. This also enables the class to build confidence in being able to work on tasks without the teacher. In a classroom involving genuine dialogue, the student is considered to be a knowledgeable and critical partner in learning (Aronowitz, 1981; Bovill, 2013; Darder et al, 2003; Freire, 2003; Shor, 1992).

Critical questions for practice

Reflecting on opportunities for dialogue within your teaching

» How do you currently enable students to bring their knowledge and experiences into class?

» What opportunities are there in your classes for dialogue?

» What further steps could you take to make connections between what is taught and students' interests and perspectives?

Co-creating learning and teaching helps to build relationships

Co-creating learning and teaching, in drawing on students' knowledge, skills and experience to negotiate learning and teaching decisions, also contributes to developing relationships between teacher and students, and between students and students. When teachers and students set out to co-create learning and teaching, the initiative can come from either the teacher or students. However, where HE systems have established the teacher as the person typically responsible for learning and teaching, it is perhaps no surprise that much co-creation of learning and teaching is led, at least initially, by teachers (Bovill, 2014). Therefore, any teacher setting out to invite students to co-create learning and teaching in a class needs to demonstrate a genuine interest in the students, a friendliness and openness that is likely to help begin the process of building relationships and establishing trust. Teachers need to demonstrate a sincere respect for students' perspectives and capabilities, as well as a willingness to negotiate learning and teaching processes (Bovill, 2019b). For some teachers, this may feel like the natural way to teach, but for many teachers this can feel quite daunting, as it differs from how university teaching is typically conceptualised.

Mercer-Mapstone et al (2017), Deeley and Bovill (2014), Deeley (2014) and Bovill et al (2010) all specifically highlight the enhanced relationships, team-working and sense of community that result from co-creation and partnership work. Bron, Bovill, Van Vliet and Veugelers (2016) report that students involved in negotiation and shared decision-making learn to become skilled negotiators. Negotiation is difficult, and students will usually not learn how to become skilled negotiators by sitting in lectures. The processes of co-creating learning and teaching offer the opportunity to practise negotiation. Sometimes, staff and students get things wrong, or find negotiation difficult, but these lessons are formative in enabling both staff and students to enhance their ability to understand different perspectives, to listen, to compromise, and to make shared decisions. These experiences are important if students are to become future citizens and active agents for change (Bron, Bovill and Veugelers, 2016). These processes of negotiation and shared decision-making also enable staff and students to develop significant and meaningful relationships based on mutual respect and shared endeavour. Asplundh (2019, p 2) describes her experience of collaborating with faculty: *'it helped me see my professors as more human'*.

Example 4.2

Even bell hooks finds some classes challenging

The African American feminist writer and teacher bell hooks is widely considered an inspiring role model for those interested in critical pedagogy and relational teaching. Sometimes, I think it is helpful when our heroes and role models admit to struggling with some of the things we all struggle with. In the following excerpt, hooks (1994, pp 158–9) describes a class that wasn't going well.

I had this class that I just hated. I hated it so bad I didn't want to get up in the morning and go to it... One of the things that fascinated me about that experience is that we failed to create a learning community in the classroom. That did not mean that individual students didn't learn a great deal, but in terms of creating a communal context for learning, it was a failure. That failure was heartbreaking for me. It was hard to accept that I was not able to control the direction our classroom was moving in. I would think, "What can I do? And what could I have done?" And I kept reminding myself that I couldn't do it alone, that forty other people were also in there.

This example starkly illustrates the necessity of building relationships in order for teaching and learning to progress. It is also

a powerful reminder that a teacher is not in sole control of what happens in any class. We need to develop a wide range of strategies if we wish to communicate our intentions to share power with students.

(Bovill, 2019b, p 11)

Education as a shared endeavour

Strong positive relationships are often built during co-creation processes because learning and teaching becomes a shared endeavour where the teacher is learning and the students often contribute to teaching. As Freire (2003, p 63) argues:

Through dialogue, the teacher-of-the-students and the students-of-the-teacher cease to exist and a new term emerges: teacher-student with students-teachers. The teacher is no longer merely the-one-who-teaches, but who is himself [sic] taught in dialogue with the students, who in turn while being taught also teach.

This overlapping and redefining of roles mean that teachers often learn as much from students as students learn from teachers (Boyd et al, 2006; De Los Reyes and Gozemba, 2002).

One common misunderstanding of co-creation is that students get everything they ask for. The term co-creation implies that this is not something that is student-led, but rather, teacher and students are colleagues in making decisions about learning and teaching together. It also does not mean that students' experience becomes more important than learning knowledge about the subject, but rather that knowledge is seen as something that can be co-constructed. The teacher and the students bring different knowledge and experiences to the classroom, and in this shared learning space, knowledge and skills are developed, but also relationships are built.

Sharing power

Co-creation requires that the power over decisions about learning and teaching is shared. This is not necessarily the case in relational pedagogy without an emphasis on co-creation. As Delpish et al (2010, p 111) observe:

students are accustomed to, and often comfortable with, assuming a relatively powerless role in the classroom, just as faculty are trained to believe that their disciplinary expertise gives them complete authority over the learning process. When faculty or students challenge these habits, students and faculty must confront fundamental questions about the nature of teaching and learning.

Co-creation changes the way we do learning and teaching in HE, and with this, the assumptions about where power in teaching and learning lies. Fielding (1999, p 21) argues for a *radical collegiality*, where '*students enter the collegium, not as objects of professional endeavour, but as partners in the learning process, and, on occasions, as teachers of teachers, not solely, or merely as perpetual learners*'.

Co-creation requires teachers to relinquish some of their power; as De Los Reyes (2002, pp 49–50) argues; '*the teacher needs to make it clear that he or she is interested in sharing power by giving students room to participate*'. This is harder than it sounds for many teachers who are used to controlling the focus and direction of classes. Breen and Littlejohn (2000, p 277) suggest '*teachers may need to come to see their own plans for classroom work as simply proposals... which learners have the right to reformulate, elaborate upon or even reject*'. New colleagues, and those on temporary or untenured contracts, may, rightly, be more nervous of changing the way they teach, due to concerns about how they will be evaluated and the impact this might have on their position. Yet, this is not about throwing out the idea of good preparation, but as Gozemba (2002b, p 72) argues, '*a teacher has to be willing to see himself or herself as a partner in education, not the master of the classroom*'.

There will always be some people who question whether power can really be shared between teacher and students due to the nature of the hierarchy in HE (Allin, 2014). MacFarlane (2004, p 124) suggests:

there is a danger here that it is only the students who are being encouraged to self-disclose details of their innermost thoughts and personal experiences. This is potentially an abuse of the unequal power relationship between the student and the lecturer.

However, this is not a description of shared responsibility and decision-making at the heart of co-creation. Certainly, we must be mindful of the traditionally unequal power relationship between students and teachers, but the examples of co-creation in this book help to illustrate that new forms of positive pedagogical relationships are possible. If you think back to the definitions in Chapter 3, I acknowledged that some colleagues are nervous of using the term partnership due to its associations with equality, and some may be concerned about how to begin to create positive relationships with students. You may find it easier to start by enhancing active learning in your teaching, and working towards building relationships and co-creation in some specific elements of your teaching. If you are unsure where to start, there are some practical suggestions in Chapter 5.

Critical questions for practice

Reflecting on sharing power in learning and teaching

» What concerns you, if anything, about sharing power with students in your teaching?

» What excites you about sharing power with students in your teaching?

» I encourage you to discuss your answers with a colleague (staff or student).

The classroom as an under-utilised opportunity for relational pedagogy and co-creation of learning and teaching

Let us consider some of the key arguments I have made so far: positive relationships are at the heart of good teaching; positive relationships are the foundation for co-creating learning and teaching; co-creating learning and teaching helps build deeper relationships; most current co-creation and partnership activity is focused on projects involving only a few students; the first encounters we have with students are critical to communicating that we intend to take a relational approach, and that we care about students and their interests and experiences.

I would like to add that:

» we are not paying enough attention to the power of whole-class co-creation in learning and teaching;

» we are not paying enough attention to relational approaches to teaching in HE; and

» each time a teacher meets a new class of students at university, whether face-to-face or online, there is an opportunity for something meaningful to happen. If you think of how many times, teachers meet new classes of students, the classroom is currently an under-utilised opportunity for relational pedagogy and co-creation of learning and teaching. Think about what might happen if even 20 per cent of these teachers were to take a relational approach to teaching.

I present here some examples of relational teaching and co-creation to help you to think about what might be possible in your practice.

Example 4.3

Initial teacher education course, Luleå University of Technology, Luleå, Sweden – Ulrika Bergmark and Susanne Westman

At Luleå University of Technology in Sweden, Associate Professor Bergmark taught two Initial Teacher Education classes with 35 students in each class. She spent time building good-quality relationships with her students to enable them to co-create the course with her. After the course, Bergmark invited her colleague Dr Westman, who did not participate in the course, to be a critical friend and co-author of a paper.

At our university, teachers are required to present a study guide (a detailed plan of course activities) two weeks before class begins. However, in order to promote student engagement, there was no completed study guide before the course started. Instead, the lead instructor posted a tentative study guide and information about the first session and invited the students to plan the course together with the teacher. Then, based on the learning goals of the course, they created assignments related to the content of the course, including the literature. The other part of creating space for student engagement was inviting the students

→

to be active participants in educational activities. This included working in study groups and using multimodality in the learning processes. For example, students were invited to illustrate learning theories through drawings. The students conducted role-plays based on student-formulated examples including their previous experiences of learning situations, in order to try out different learning theories in a fictitious situation.

(Bergmark and Westman, 2016, p 32)

Example 4.4

Relational pedagogy and co-creation at University College Northern Denmark – Louise Esko Refshøj and Steffen Holme Helledie

At University College Northern Denmark (UCN), Louise Esko Refshøj and Steffen Holme Helledie teach an 18-month 'Top Up' programme, which leads to a Bachelors in Innovation and Entrepreneurship, to 50 students each year. They emphasise building meaningful relationships with students and opportunities to co-create learning and teaching. One of the ways they emphasise peer relationships in class is to encourage each student to put a picture of themselves on the classroom wall with information about things that each student thinks they are good at and which other students should feel able to approach them about if they want help in that area. This celebrates the skills and attributes students have, as well as practically offering support to students who might need help in those areas during the course. Before the course begins, the teachers create a shared PowerPoint slides file and they ask the students to contribute some text or pictures illustrating what they think innovation is. Then as the course progresses, each time the class meets, some of the slides are shown and whoever is responsible for the slides needs to explain them. An unexpected result of this approach was that class attendance was fantastic, because they used different numbers of slides each week depending on how the class progressed, and so students did not know when their slides might appear and when they would need to be there.

Example 4.5

Co-navigation of a course at Edinburgh Napier University, Scotland, UK – Mark Huxham

Mark Huxham (along with Megan Hunter, Robyn Shilland and Angela McIntyre, three students in his class, and Jan McArthur, an expert advisor) describe teaching an ecology class of 35 fourth-year students. They refer to their work as '*a series of attempts to imagine the curriculum and our relationships in different ways*' (Huxham et al, 2015, p 531). In contrast to many courses that are pre-defined, Huxham and colleagues used mountaineering metaphors to describe the students as '*co-navigators*' of the course, '*moving forwards*' (p 531) as the course developed and progressed. They also experimented with teaching spaces, taking some classes outdoors and experiencing how this influenced the teaching and learning that resulted. They argue that '*the principles – of mutual respect, genuine sharing of control and rethinking the parameters of time and space to suit what is most appropriate for the type of knowledge students are engaging with – could apply in most disciplinary areas*' (p 540). Ultimately, this relational co-creational approach is about adapting and developing a new approach to teaching. One powerful element of this work was focused on the assessment for the course. Huxham was proud of the 'fake paper' he had developed over a number of years, containing a series of cunning deliberate mistakes, designed specifically for the students to critique. He even designed a journal cover page and logo (*Journal of Eclectic Research*). He was then understandably a little disgruntled when the students told him very clearly that they wanted to read and critique real papers not phoney ones. With the benefit of hindsight, he realised that his students had co-designed a more authentic and more challenging assessment.

Example 4.6

An efficacy-centred approach to online teaching – Manda Williamson, University of Nebraska, USA

Dr Williamson teaches an online 'Introduction to Psychology' course for 700 students in which she encourages students to build relationships with her and other students as well as providing opportunities to share decisions about the course. She makes it explicit that she uses efficacy interventions, which have

→

been well evidenced in psychological research. She sends the students a letter to introduce herself and share her expectations of them, and she states that she is confident that with hard work and persistence, they will succeed. She repeats versions of this message in all her correspondence with students, emphasising they belong and can succeed. She invites the students to decide what the class exam average grade should be. She then includes a discussion forum online for students to collaborate to reach the student-established class exam average. They co-create study guides, and post useful resources such as videos describing key concepts and they also encourage each other by sharing motivational memes. Students who successfully complete the course with a B+ or greater are invited to work in the Introduction to Psychology Tutoring Center. They assist current students with the course assignments, study skills, and they grade written assignments. These students volunteer and are offered independent study credit and a letter of recommendation by Dr Williamson. The course has twice the rate of student success of previous versions of the same course as well as other comparable face-to-face courses (Felten and Lambert, 2020; Williamson, 2020).

Summary

- There is a two-way, mutually reinforcing, connection between positive relationships and co-creating learning and teaching. First, positive relationships are foundational for co-creating learning and teaching. Second, co-creating learning and teaching builds positive teacher–student and student–student relationships.

- Relationships and whole-class co-created learning and teaching are inextricably linked but currently there is little research pulling these ideas together.

- Early encounters between teachers and students are key in establishing a learning environment that communicates the teacher's intention to students, and opens the opportunity for building relationships and trust.

- Teachers meet new classes of students face to face and online regularly, but these opportunities are currently an under-utilised opportunity for relationship building in HE.

Useful texts

Bovill, C (2019b) Co-Creation in Learning and Teaching: The Case for a Whole-Class Approach in Higher Education. *Higher Education.* [online] Available at: https://link.springer.com/article/10.1007/s10734-019-00453-w (accessed 12 January 2020).

In this article, I provide an overview of how current co-creation and partnership work focuses predominantly on project-based partnerships involving a few selected students. I make the case for involving all students in whole-class co-creation in learning and teaching and for the key role of relationships in co-creation.

Lubicz-Nawrocka, T (2016) *Co-creation of the Curriculum and Social Justice: Changing the Nature of Student-Teacher Relationships in Higher Education.* Lancaster University. Paper presented at Higher Education Close Up (HECU) conference, 18–20 July. [online] Available at: www.lancaster.ac.uk/fass/events/hecu8/papers/Lubicz.pdf (accessed 12 January 2020).

This conference paper reports on research into examples of co-creation of the curriculum in Scotland, arguing for the benefits of co-creation in developing positive relationships and more socially just education and outcomes.

Chapter 5 | What does this mean for my teaching practice?

The classroom remains the most radical space of possibility in the academy.

(hooks, 1994, p 12)

Introduction

How often do we maximise the possibility of the face-to-face and online classrooms we teach in? In the previous chapter, I argued that when teachers meet students in classrooms for the first time, they have an important opportunity to set the tone for learning and teaching, and begin to establish positive relationships, and currently I think this is an under-utilised opportunity. Perhaps being aware of this opportunity is, in itself, a step towards relational approaches to teaching, but being aware does not necessarily mean that it is easy for teachers to adopt relational approaches to teaching, such as co-creation. This chapter aims to provide answers to practical questions that you might have about how to proceed.

What steps can I take towards relational teaching?

Put time into planning your first class, because what you do in the first class sends a strong signal to students about how you wish your classroom to function. Think about the following questions in planning your first class:

>> How will you welcome the students?

>> How can you get your students talking and interacting?

>> How can you communicate to your students that they matter to you?

It can be worth spending time welcoming students. Greet them as they enter the class-room. Consider devoting time to an early exercise where students get to know one another and you get to know your students a little better. For example, ask students to share in pairs their name and one thing about themselves they are happy to share but that not many people know about them, and ask those students who are willing to share with the class. Or perhaps you can ask students what they like to do on a Saturday afternoon, or their favourite TV programme and why. Each of these ideas are simple ice-breakers to get students talking and to share a little of themselves. It is also important to signal that you are willing to share a little of yourself. Think also about whether there are personal experiences you can share during the course that help illustrate some real examples relevant to the course. This is not an excuse to constantly talk about yourself, but students usually appreciate being able to see their teacher as human. '*Stories told from a teacher to her students... are exercises in building empathy, and immensely effective ways to communicate a lesson through connection*' (Damon, 2018, p 41). Take care to ensure that you build upon the getting-to-know-you exercises in the following weeks. Think how you can make connections to your students' interests. Try not to use one of these introductory exercises and then continue to deliver lectures for the next ten weeks.

Find opportunities to talk to your students. Even in large classes, if you break up teaching with group work, wander around and talk to students. If you are posing questions in class, move around to try to speak more closely with students rather than always standing at the front of the room in one place. Encourage students to offer their ideas on a white board at the front or sides of the room. This can help students to feel that their ideas are valued. But be mindful if asking students to do this in large classes where they may feel uncomfortable in front of so many peers. Think about ways of sharing who is speaking or teaching in online settings – maybe you could invite students to present their ideas or to use virtual pens to annotate slides.

Try to remember your students' names. Consider using sticky labels for students to put their names on, or in larger classes, students can make simple name tents to place on their desk (as mentioned in Chapter 2), or they can put their names in big letters on the back of their laptops, so when they have their laptops open in a lecture theatre it is easy to see who is who. Try to use students' names when you ask questions or to thank students for contributions, and even if you don't know a student's name, ask for their name before you talk with them.

Where do I start if I want to co-create learning and teaching?

The first steps towards a new way of doing learning and teaching *with* students can feel daunting, so it is worth considering advice from Cook-Sather et al (2014) on establishing partnerships.

> » *Start small*: if you are teaching a smaller class you could try co-creation with this class first. Or could you think about co-creating one element of the teaching, eg one of the teaching exercises, or one assignment? It doesn't have to be large-scale co-creation from day one.

» *Be patient*: things do not always go to plan. You may be new to this approach, but you may need to be patient with some of your students who may also be new to this approach. Evidence suggests that the rewards of being patient and persisting with negotiating elements of learning and teaching will pay dividends.

» *Invite participation*: obliging students to co-create with you is likely to back-fire as a strategy and seems at odds with the underpinning ethos of learning and teaching done *with* students. However, different students may want to engage in a variety of ways, so it is worth planning for the possibility that not all students will be positive about co-creation when you first suggest it. Having a plan B and a plan C and recognising students' different interests can help you to be ready for suggesting a range of opportunities. Be enthu-siastic, and if possible have different ways students can be involved, encourage questions and suggestions – often this leads to students wanting to co-create.

» *Work together to create a shared purpose and project*: are there any of the course assignments that could be created as a group assignment? Are there elements of the course content that could be defined or investigated by the class? Creating group projects can help to establish a shared group purpose that can help the group support one another and start to co-create together. In some contexts, it can feel appropriate to establish shared group rules and aims.

» *Cultivate support*: often there are other people who are interested in, informed about, or experienced in, co-creating learning and teaching. Try to connect with others who can act as allies, mentors or supportive colleagues to help you work out different ways you can approach your work, or how to deal with a thorny problem. Also try to cultivate support from senior people in your institution for co-creating learning and teaching. Does your Centre for Academic Development offer any funding to support your work? Is there interest in co-creation from senior managers? Would they be interested in the evidence of the benefits from co-creation? Gaining support can help you to feel that your work is valued and you might be able to get practical help such as a student teaching assistant to help you co-create a class.

» *Learn from mistakes*: things do not always go right the first time. However, we can usually learn a great deal when things do not go to plan. Try not to give up, but to be open to see how you might do things differently the next time.

One easy approach which you could try as a first step towards co-creation is to use 'the missing perspective'. This approach *'is based on the teacher leaving a scheduled session towards the end of the course unplanned. It is then the students' task to fill this session with a perspective they think has been missing in the course'* (Barrineau et al, 2019, p 96). Some teachers will feel the pressure of covering vast amounts of content in their course and the idea of leaving a session blank may at first seem impossible, but many curriculum experts argue that we focus too much on content and that we do not spend enough time on learning key concepts and developing skills. The missing perspective is a light-touch way of starting to signal to students some shared responsibility for learning and teaching.

Shor (1992, p 158) describes trying to learn to share responsibility with students:

To reassure students, I arrive with meaningful exercises and enough structure to give the class direction. I invite their questions about the subject matter and class requirements... students are not expecting a democratic classroom and are not prepared to co-govern all at once... I have to provide a democratic structure and invite them into it step by step.

What do I do if I teach a large class?

For many teachers, teaching large classes may not be negotiable. This said, it is worth lobbying in all suitable settings to reduce class sizes, using the robust research evidence of poorer student outcomes from large classes to support your arguments. Victoria University, in Melbourne, Australia have introduced what they call *First Year College*. They have adapted the whole of their first-year course structure and hired more faculty and teaching assistants to ensure that all first-year classes are now much smaller. The College enables students to work *'closely with academic teaching staff, with a smaller group of peers, on one unit and its assessment tasks at a time (over a four week block)'* (Victoria University, 2019). This approach recognises the value of reducing class sizes. One colleague from Victoria University I spoke with claimed that the money saved from students dropping out and needing support services pays for the additional teaching assistants and support needed, with money left over.

However, I realise that we still need to think about how to create more relational approaches and co-creation in the large classes that currently exist. I mentioned in Chapter 3 that most of the examples of co-creating learning and teaching with a whole class of students tend to come from classes of approximately 50 students or less. Yet there are some great examples of how teachers are making large classes more engaging (see Examples 3.5, 3.6, 4.1 and 4.6). I raised the question in Chapter 3 whether students just have more choice in larger classes rather than them being engaged in significant co-creation, but even students having a limited choice from prescribed choices (see the Ladder of student participation in curriculum design in Chapter 3) can still mean that they are involved to some extent in shared decision-making.

One powerful approach is to try to create the sense of smaller classes within the larger class. This can be done by using small group work (even in steep lecture theatres with fixed seating, students can usually talk in groups of three to five). Volunteers can be invited to the front of the class to share work from small groups. If a teacher provides three or four different problems to solve or case studies to discuss, maybe different parts of the room could bid to solve a particular problem or case and then present their ideas back to the whole class. These scenarios involve a little choice and increased responsibility from students. Another idea is to get students to do work online in smaller groups in between classes; then when they are in class, ask students to sit next to their small group members. When problems are posed in class, the group is already formed to work together. This is a great way of students getting to know one another and helping them to feel they belong.

In larger classes, technology can be a big help. Electronic voting technology can enable students to feel that they are getting more involved. Try to include some questions that enable students to vote on the direction of the course or help you to adapt your teaching to be more responsive and relevant. Try using contemporary connections to current affairs and popular culture and getting students to speak about their answers in groups. The software *Peerwise* can be used to get students to author multiple choice questions (MCQs) and write correct answers as well as explanations about why the other answer options are incorrect. Students then answer each other's questions and rate them for quality. Students learn more about the subject by having to construct questions and good-quality distractor answers, and find *Peerwise* to be a rich resource for revision (Cook-Sather et al, 2014).

Another idea for building peer relationships in large lectures is a note-taking relay. The teacher breaks after approximately 20 minutes, when the students have a couple of minutes to write down what they think were the most important ideas from the first 20 minutes. The students then pass their note to the student sitting next to them. After another 20 minutes this is repeated. At the end of the lecture, this can be repeated again and students can keep the last note, and earlier notes from their neighbours (Engström in Barrineau et al, 2019). For another example of collaboration in a large class, see Example 2.2 in Chapter 2 about two-stage examinations.

How do I share decision-making without causing mayhem?

If we try to adopt relational teaching or to co-create learning and teaching, some teachers become concerned about what might happen. As bell hooks (1994, p 152) describes:

the bottom-line assumption has to be that everyone in the classroom is able to act responsibly. That has to be the starting point – that we are able to act responsibly together to create a learning environment. All too often we have been trained as professors to assume students are not capable of acting responsibly, that if we don't exert control over them, then there's just going to be mayhem.

These concerns are based upon low expectations of students. In many examples of co-creation we actually see the opposite: students exceed our expectations (Bovill, 2014). However, turning up on the first day with no plan and saying we're going to co-create the class may cause mayhem, because students are unclear what is expected of them or how to proceed. They can also be legitimately worried about wasting time, fairness and their need to graduate. We need to provide a plan, a flexible outline of ideas, but which clearly communicates to students what we are aiming to achieve and why, a warm invitation for them to be part of defining and co-creating the class, and suggestions of how to move forward.

It does not mean it will be easy, and sometimes the energy within a group of students can surpass the teacher's energy levels. *When students codevelop themes for study and share in the making of the syllabus, the class dialogue sometimes moves faster than I can understand it or organize it for academic study.* (Shor, 1992, p 5) However, when co-creating learning and teaching, it becomes easier to ask students: would anyone like to help keep track of this conversation, or the key action points we have agreed? In a classroom where positive relationships have been built, admitting to students that we feel a little overwhelmed is often seen as an invitation for students to help – because learning and teaching has become a shared endeavour. We just need to become more comfortable admitting when we are vulnerable or need help.

What can I do if students seem disengaged?

Barrineau et al (2019, p 7) describe their idealism about setting out to co-create learning and teaching: '*That vision vanished rather quickly as we realised that, on the whole, the groups of students with which we were trying to engage were not about to line up outside of our office*'. One of the most powerful things to do if you are not sure how to engage students, or whether what you are doing is engaging students, is to ask them whether they are engaged, or what engages them. It is sometimes possible to ask students, prior to a course, what would engage them and what they have found engaging in other courses. However, remember that you may receive as many different answers as there are students in your class; we need to be careful of not assuming all students will want the same thing.

We also need to be careful not to assume students are disengaged. Just because a student does not speak up in class does not mean they are disengaged; they may be a quiet, reflective learner. Ask yourself whether the room layout or the way you ask questions or set up group work might lead some students to contribute less. We also need to be careful of labelling a student or a group of students as disengaged as if it is their fault. Often students disengage because of things we do or because of things we don't do which we should be doing. Sometimes students can't engage for some reason: perhaps they are working long hours or they have caring responsibilities. The key to unlocking our understanding of what is going on is to talk to, and build relationships with, students.

Students need teachers to be intentional in setting high expectations, letting them know we believe they can be successful and that we will support them on their journey to reaching their aspirations.

(Fisher et al, 2018, p 143)

Critical questions for practice

Reflection on the ways we talk about students

When you and your colleagues discuss students and student learning, how often are students talked about in a negative way? *They're lazy; they just don't get it, despite me explaining it clearly; they don't even come to collect the feedback I spent time writing...*

» What are the other possible explanations for their behaviour?

» What role does our teaching approach or style of communication have on these issues?

» What do you think would happen if we talked about students in more positive ways?

» What if we tried to learn from the engaged students? What do they do and how do we help all students to do what they are doing?

Wilson et al (2020) outline students' roles in Scholarship of Teaching and Leaning (SoTL) work. They urge us to consider switching from constantly having to justify the inclusion of students in SoTL work and conferences,

$\longrightarrow$

towards asking where the students are in the rest of SoTL work. This helpful switch of thinking and language can go some way to redress deficit views of students and deficit views of partnership work.

What can I do if my colleagues seem disengaged?

Some of us are fortunate to work with colleagues who are also keen to try relational approaches to teaching or to co-create learning and teaching. However, you might be in a context where your colleagues are resistant to relational approaches. This can be challenging and can make you feel isolated. Therefore, it is important to reach out to others who are already teaching in relational ways. Perhaps your university's Centre for Academic Development can put you in touch with some other teachers who have a similar outlook to you. Find allies who can help you to feel less isolated. If you are struggling to find allies at your own university, you might also look for the growing number of people interested in relational teaching and co-creation online or at conferences.

There is also a good deal of evidence in this book about why relational teaching is important for us to take seriously. Could you present some of this evidence at your School's Teaching Committee or at a lunch meeting in your department? Centres for Academic Development may host events about relational teaching, in which case could you invite a colleague to join you, who might not otherwise go, and maybe you could schedule a coffee with them after the event to discuss it. As with concerns about student engagement, when there are concerns about staff engagement, one of the best approaches is to ask staff if they are interested or engaged in relational teaching and why. Ask them how their current teaching is going and share with them some of the research findings supporting the importance of building relationships. Ask them when they have been most engaged with teaching. These questions might open up a useful conversation.

How do I prevent myself from slipping back into old teaching habits?

If you have some success at building relationships with your students or co-creating learning and teaching, you may have experienced the positive rewards associated with these practices. Yet, it can seem challenging not only in the early stages to change your teaching practices, but also to sustain relational teaching as a way you continue to teach.

Allin (2014, p 99) demonstrates the need for continual self-critique, in the multiple questions she asks herself about the partnership approach she tried with students focused on co-research:

I began to reflect further on my project... Had I been manipulative in order to ensure a good level of data collection? Was my 'collaboration' with students merely cursory? Were the interpretations more mine than the students? How did power differentials and my assumptions about students as researchers manifest themselves? How did this affect the potential learning from the project? Why does it matter?

This level of critique and reflection can support you to push further in developing and honing your relational teaching. Newell Decyk et al (2010, p 59), also discussing co-inquiry with students in a SoTL project, highlight some of the challenges of sustaining co-creation:

Trust, especially new trust, is fragile. The excitement and energy that initially goes into a SoTL co-inquiry group can wane when people assume new responsibilities or commitments. Old habits of power and passivity die hard. Faculty may change positions or retire. Students graduate. Sustaining co-inquiry as a viable research approach in SoTL takes vigilance and effort.

It can be helpful in these situations to take time to revisit your original aspirations.

Try to remain constructively critical of your own practice, through reflection, through conversations with colleagues, and through conversations with students (Jarvis and Clark, 2020; Roxå and Mårtensson, 2009). You will not always get it right, but if you are motivated to try to adopt a more relational approach to teaching, the chances are your students will notice and you may well get feedback that encourages you to keep pushing for more meaningful and democratic approaches to teaching.

Summary

- In this chapter, I have attempted to respond to a range of practical questions about co-creation and relational teaching.

- I recommend reflecting on these responses, as well as having conversations with colleagues, as ways to enhance understanding and build confidence in your practice.

$\longrightarrow$

- If relational teaching and co-creation feel different from your usual approach to teaching, it may be challenging to implement these new approaches at first.

- But taking small steps, and finding allies can be helpful in implementing and sustaining these more engaged forms of teaching.

Useful texts

Cook-Sather, A, Bovill, C and Felten, P (2014) *Engaging Students as Partners in Learning and Teaching: A Guide for Faculty*. San Francisco: Jossey Bass.

There are two chapters of this book which answer a range of common questions about student–faculty partnerships, and which you might find helpful if you have further questions about co-creation: Chapter 2 'Preliminary Questions about Student–Faculty Partnerships (pp 15–26) and Chapter 8 'Further Questions about Student–Faculty Partnerships' (pp 171–85).

teachers together can give them more confidence to push further with the work they are doing, and as they gain confidence, they can be powerful advocates for colleagues who are helped by seeing what is possible. Ultimately, academic developers need to offer support to teachers as they attempt to implement relational pedagogy and co-creation. They also need to support and advise senior managers in designing and implementing strategies and policies that will create a culture promoting relational pedagogy and co-creation across universities.

Implications for senior managers

A public commitment to relational pedagogy and co-creation can be powerful. For example, in work taking place at the University of Edinburgh to envision the future of university digital education:

relationships, dialogues and personal exchanges between students and staff build understanding in a way that is not possible via transmissive forms of teaching. Teaching should be designed to provide the time and space for proper relationships and meaningful human exchange.

(University of Edinburgh, 2019, p 15)

This work explicitly highlights the importance of '*prioritising human contact and relationships*' (p 19) and the use of co-design methodologies and enhanced student agency. If you are a senior manager within a university, you can support relational pedagogy and co-creation by making public statements like this. Even more powerful is if you can match this public statement with a commitment to resources to support the changes that are needed to make relational teaching a reality.

Chambliss and Takacs (2014, p 68) introduce the concept of '*the arithmetic of engagement*', which suggests that:

at any particular moment, there are a limited number of great opportunities for students to become engaged. Fortunately, however, even a small number of engaging people and events, properly located, can have a disproportionately positive impact... out of perhaps twenty-five teachers a student has during college, she needs only one or two 'great' ones to feel that she has had an excellent academic experience. In a small college, a tiny number (say, five or ten) of excellent large courses can positively affect large numbers of students. Conversely, a single poor professor, teaching a large introductory course can easily destroy scores of students' interest in a discipline.

However, we must also take seriously the need to reduce class sizes. Large classes lead to poorer student outcomes (Cuseo, 2007; Gibbs, 2010 and 2012) and make it harder to adopt relational teaching and co-creation approaches. This will require resources, particularly more teaching staff, but as Victoria University in Melbourne discovered (see Chapter 5), it is a worthwhile investment.

Support for raising the status of teaching within recruitment and promotion processes is also needed. Unless colleagues think teaching is taken seriously, they will not invest their time in trying to enhance teaching. Mayhew et al (2016, p 594) argue that:

Another way to spur good teaching practice is to provide the necessary support for the growing number of centers for teaching and learning/faculty excellence/faculty development. To a small but significant degree, these support centers have been linked to student intellectual and cognitive development. These services often serve as the hub where instructors discuss pedagogical innovation, test and reflect on new teaching techniques... in all cases, educating the educators will require institutional leaders' commitment to reframe the discourse and value of teaching.

Final thoughts

This book has brought together research on relational pedagogy and co-creation of learning and teaching. While I have provided evidence and examples to support you to think about what might be possible in your practice, we need further research and examples of whole-class co-creation and relational approaches to continue to highlight what is possible. I hope that the book has provided you with ideas and inspiration to consider introducing or extending a relational or co-creation approach with your students. Changing the way we teach across HE requires a significant culture shift. A culture shift will not happen overnight, but we can each play a part in contributing to more positive student experiences at university by adopting more relational approaches to teaching.

This book has also attempted to highlight the importance of whole-class co-creation. I highlighted earlier in this chapter Mayhew and colleagues' claim that classroom educators have the largest impact on student learning. This is perhaps not surprising, but the potential of classroom and online class teaching to include all students in relationship building and shared decision-making is an incredible opportunity we must maximise. Building positive relationships will support co-creation in learning and teaching, and co-creation can enhance relationships further as well as increasing students' skills in negotiation. Each time we meet a new class of students, we have an important opportunity. If you already pay attention to building relationships with your students, you are likely to be making an important contribution to positive student experiences. If you haven't really paid attention to relationships before, in your next class, try to demonstrate to students that you are interested to get to know them, try to learn their names, and think of ways you can show that you care about them, and see what happens...

References

Allin, L (2014) Collaboration Between Staff and Students in the Scholarship of Teaching and Learning: The Potential and the Problems. *Teaching and Learning Inquiry*, 2: 95–102.

Apple, M W (1981) On Analysing Hegemony. In Giroux, H A, Penna, A N and Pinar, W F (eds) *Curriculum and Instruction Alternatives in Education*. Berkeley: McCutchen Publishing.

Arnstein, S R (1969) A Ladder of Citizen Participation. *Journal of the American Institute of Planners*, 35: 216–24.

Aronowitz, S (1981) Politics and Higher Education in the 1980s. In Giroux, H A, Penna, A N and Pinar, W F (eds) *Curriculum and Instruction Alternatives in Education*. Berkeley: McCutchen Publishing.

Arum, R and Roksa, J (2011) *Academically Adrift: Limited Learning on College Campuses*. Chicago: University of Chicago Press.

Asplundh, M (2019) An Autobiography of Becoming: Community, Mentorship, and Partnership as a Means for Self-Realization. *Teaching and Learning Together in Higher Education*, 26: 1–3.

Astin, A W (1977) *Four Critical Years: Effects of College on Beliefs, Attitudes, and Knowledge*. San Francisco: Jossey Bass.

Astin, A W (1993) *What Matters in College? Four Critical Years Revised*. San Francisco: Jossey-Bass.

Baik, C, Larcombe, W and Brooker, A (2019) How Universities Can Enhance Student Mental Wellbeing: The Student Perspective. *Higher Education Research and Development*. [online] Available at: doi.org/10.1080/07294360.2019.1576596 (accessed 12 January 2020).

Barrineau, S, Engström, A and Schnaas, U (2019) *An Active Student Participation Companion*. Uppsala: Uppsala University. [online] Available at: www.diva-portal.org/smash/get/diva2:1286438/FULLTEXT02.pdf (accessed 12 January 2020).

Beard, C, Clegg, S and Smith, K (2007) Acknowledging the Affective in Higher Education. *British Educational Research Journal*, 33: 235–52.

Bergmark, U and Westman, S (2016) Co-Creating Curriculum in Higher Education: Promoting Democratic Values and a Multidimensional View on Learning. *International Journal for Academic Development*, 21: 28–40.

Biesta, G J J (2006) *Beyond Learning: Democratic Education for a Human Future*. London: Paradigm Publishers.

Biesta, G, Bingham, C, Hutchison, J N, McDaniel, B L, Margonis, F, Mayo, C, Pijanowski, C M, Romano, R M, Sidorkin, A M, Stengel, B S and Thayer-Bacon, B J (2010) Manifesto of Relational Pedagogy: Meeting to Learning, Learning to Meet. A Joint Contribution by All Authors. In Bingham, C and Sidorkin A M (eds) *No Education Without Relation*. New York: Peter Lang Publishing.

Bingham, C (2010) Let's Treat Authority Relationally. In Bingham, C and Sidorkin A M (eds) *No Education Without Relation*. New York: Peter Lang Publishing.

Bingham, C and Sidorkin, A M (2010) Introduction. In Bingham, C and Sidorkin A M (eds) *No Education Without Relation*. New York: Peter Lang Publishing.

Bonwell, C C and Eison, J A (1991) *Active Learning: Creating Excitement in the Classroom*. Washington DC: George Washington University.

Boomer, G (1982) *Negotiating the Curriculum: A Teacher-Student Partnership*. Sydney: Asthon Scholastic.

Boomer, G, Lester, N, Onore, C and Cook, J (1992) *Negotiating the Curriculum: Educating for the 21st Century*. London: The Falmer Press.

Bovill, C (2013) Students and Staff Co-Creating Curricula – A New Trend or an Old Idea We Never Got Around to Implementing? In Rust, C (ed) *Improving Student Learning Through Research and Scholarship: 20 Years of ISL*. Oxford: The Oxford Centre for Staff and Educational Development.

Bovill, C (2014) An Investigation of Co-Created Curricula Within Higher Education in the UK, Ireland and the USA. *Innovations in Education and Teaching International*, 51: 15–25.

Bovill, C (2015) *Identifying Your Underlying Assumptions in Co-Creating Learning and Teaching: The Importance of Language and Behaviour.* University of Cambridge. Paper presented at Student Voice Conference, 22–24 June.

Bovill, C (2017a) A Framework to Explore Roles Within Student-Staff Partnerships in Higher Education: Which Students are Partners, When and in What Ways? *International Journal for Students as Partners*, 1: 1–5. [online] Available at: doi.org/10.15173.ijsap.v1i1.3062 (accessed 12 January 2020).

Bovill, C (2017b) *Decision-Making in Co-Created Learning and Teaching: Responding to Calls to BYOS (Bring Your Own Student).* Celtic Manor Hotel, Newport. Paper presented at Society for Research in Higher Education Conference, 6–8 December.

Bovill, C (2018) Decision Making in Partnership: Tools to Support Partnership Planning. In Bryson C and Flint A (eds) Proceedings of the RAISE International Colloquium on Partnership June 23, Birmingham City University. *Student Engagement in Higher Education Journal*, 2: 110–11. [online] Available at: journals.gre.ac.uk/index.php/raise/article/view/Bryson (accessed 12 January 2020).

Bovill, C (2019a) A Co-Creation of Learning and Teaching Typology: What Kind of Co-Creation are you Planning or Doing? *International Journal for Students as Partners*, 3: 91–8. [online] Available at: doi.org/10.15173/ijsap.v3i2.3953 (accessed 12 January 2020).

Bovill, C (2019b) Co-Creation in Learning and Teaching: The Case for a Whole-Class Approach in Higher Education. *Higher Education.* [online] Available at: link.springer.com/article/10.1007/s10734-019-00453-w (accessed 12 January 2020).

Bovill, C (2019c) Staff-Student Partnerships in Learning and Teaching: An Overview of Current Practice and Discourse. *Journal of Geography in Higher Education*, 43: 385–98.

Bovill, C, Aitken, G, Hutchison, J, Morrison, F, Roseweir, K, Scott, A and Sotannde, S (2010) Experiences of Learning through Collaborative Evaluation from a Postgraduate Certificate in Professional Education. *International Journal for Academic Development*, 15: 143–54.

Bovill, C and Bulley, C J (2011) A Model of Active Student Participation in Curriculum Design: Exploring Desirability and Possibility. In Rust, C (ed) *Improving Student Learning (ISL) 18; Global Theories and Local Practices: Institutional, Disciplinary and Cultural Variations* (pp 176–88). Series: Improving Student Learning (18). Oxford: Oxford Brookes University, Oxford Centre for Staff and Learning Development (pp 176–88). ISBN 978 1873576809. Available at: www.brookes.ac.uk/ocsld/publications/

Bovill, C, Cook-Sather, A and Felten, P (2011) Students as Co-Creators of Teaching Approaches, Course Design, and Curricula: Implications for Academic Developers. *International Journal for Academic Development*, 16: 133–45.

Bovill, C, Cook-Sather, A, Felten, P, Millard, L and Moore-Cherry, N (2016) Addressing Potential Challenges in Co-Creating Learning and Teaching: Overcoming Resistance, Navigating Institutional Norms and Ensuring Inclusivity in Student-Staff Partnerships. *Higher Education*, 71: 195–208.

Bovill, C, Morss, K and Bulley, C (2009) Should Students Participate in Curriculum Design? Discussion Arising from a First Year Curriculum Design Project and a Literature Review. *Pedagogical Research in Maximising Education*, 3: 17–26.

Bovill, C and Woolmer, C (2019) How Conceptualisations of Curriculum in Higher Education Influence Student-Staff Co-Creation *in* and *of* the Curriculum. *Higher Education*, 78: 407–22.

Boyd, R, MacNeill, N and Sullivan, G (2006) Relational Pedagogy, Putting Balance Back into Students' Learning. *Curriculum and Leadership Journal*, 4. [online] Available at: cmslive.curriculum.edu.au/leader/default.asp?id=13944andissueID=10277 (accessed 12 January 2020).

Breen, M P and Littlejohn, A (2000) The Practicalities of Negotiation. In Breen M P and Littlejohn, A (eds) *Classroom Decision-Making: Negotiation and Process Syllabuses in Practice.* Cambridge: Cambridge University Press.

Bron, J, Bovill, C, Van Vliet, E and Veugelers, W (2016) "Negotiating the Curriculum": Realizing Student Voice. *The Social Educator: Journal of the Social and Citizenship Education Association of Australia*, 34: 39–54.

Bron, J, Bovill, C and Veugelers, W (2016) Students Experiencing and Developing Democratic Citizenship Through Curriculum Negotiation: The Relevance of Garth Boomer's Approach. *Curriculum Perspectives*, 36: 15–27.

Bron, J, Bovill, C and Veugelers, W (2018) Distributed Curriculum Leadership: How Negotiation Between Student and Teacher Improves the Curriculum. *Journal of Ethical Educational Leadership*, Special Issue 1: 76–98.

Bron, J and Veugelers, W (2014) Why We Need to Involve Our Students in Curriculum Design: Five Arguments for Student Voice. *Curriculum and Teaching Dialogue*, 16: 125–39.

Brownell, J E and Swaner, L E (2010) *Five High-Impact Practices: Research on Learning Outcomes, Completion and Quality.* Washington, DC: Association of American Colleges and Universities.

Bryson, C (2014) Clarifying the Concept of Student Engagement. In Bryson, C (ed) *Understanding and Developing Student Engagement.* Abingdon: Routledge.

Bryson, C, Furlonger, R and Rinaldo-Langridge, F (2015) *A Critical Consideration of, and Research Agenda for, the Approach of 'Students as Partners'.* Ljubljana, Slovenia. Paper presented at International Conference on Improving University Teaching, 15–17 July.

Buckley, A (2014) How Radical is Student Engagement? (And What is it for?) *Student Engagement and Experience Journal*, 3. [online] Available at: doi.org/10.7190/seej.v3i2.95 (accessed 12 January 2020).

Carruthers Thomas, K (2019) *Rethinking Student Belonging in Higher Education: From Bourdieu to Borderlands.* Abingdon: Routledge.

Chambliss, D F and Takacs, C G (2014) *How College Works.* Cambridge, MA: Harvard University Press.

Chickering, A W and Gamson, Z F (1987) Seven Principles for Good Practice in Undergraduate Education. *AAHE Bulletin*, 3: 3–7.

Cook-Sather, A (2010) Students as Learners and Teachers: Taking Responsibility, Transforming Education, and Redefining Accountability. *Curriculum Inquiry*, 40: 555–75.

Cook-Sather, A (2018) Listening to Equity-Seeking Perspectives: How Students' Experiences of Pedagogical Partnership Can Inform Wider Discussions of Student Success. *Higher Education Research and Development*, 37: 923–36.

Cook-Sather, A, Bovill, C and Felten, P (2014) *Engaging Students as Partners in Learning and Teaching: A Guide for Faculty.* San Francisco: Jossey Bass.

Cook-Sather, A and Felten, P (2017) Ethics of Academic Leadership: Guiding Learning and Teaching. In Su, F and Wood, M (eds) *Cosmopolitan Perspectives on Academic Leadership in Higher Education.* London: Bloomsbury.

Cook-Sather, A, Krishna-Prasad, S, Marquis, E and Ntem, A (2019) Mobilizing a Culture Shift on Campus: Underrepresented Students as Educational Developers. *New Directions for Teaching and Learning*, 159: 21–30.

Cooper, K M, Haney, B, Krieg, A and Brownell, S E (2017) What's in a Name? The Importance of Students Perceiving that an Instructor Knows Their Names in a High-Enrollment Biology Classroom. *CBE-Life Sciences Education*, 16: 1–13.

Cranton, P (2001) *Becoming an Authentic Teacher in Higher Education.* Malabar: Krieger Publishing Company.

Cuba, L, Jennings, N, Lovett, S and Swingle, J (2016) *Making Decisions in College: Practice for Life.* Cambridge, MA: Harvard University Press.

Cuffe, R (2019) *University Teaching Grades Invalid, Statistics Body Says.* BBC News, 6 March. [online] Available at: www.bbc.co.uk/news/education-47462273 (accessed 12 January 2020).

Cuseo, J (2007) The Empirical Case Against Large Class Size: Adverse Effects on the Teaching, Learning and Retention of First-Year Students. *The Journal of Faculty Development*, 21: 5–21.

Damon, N (2018) *Time to Teach, Time to Reach: Expert Teachers Give Voice to The Power of Relational Teaching.* Cambridge: Relational Schools Foundation.

Darder, A, Baltodano, M and Torres, R D (2003) Critical Pedagogy: An Introduction. In Darder, A, Baltodano, M and Torres, R D (eds) *The Critical Pedagogy Reader.* New York: Routledge.

De Los Reyes, E (2002) Breaking the Cycle, Rising to Question: The Language Intensive Interdisciplinary Program. In De Los Reyes, E and Gozemba, P A (eds) *Pockets of Hope: How Students and Teachers Change the World.* London: Bergin and Garvey.

De Los Reyes, E and Gozemba, P A (2002) Introduction: Education as the Practice of Freedom. In De Los Reyes, E and Gozemba, P A (eds) *Pockets of Hope: How Students and Teachers Change the World.* London: Bergin and Garvey.

Deeley, S J (2014) Summative Co-Assessment: A Deep Learning Approach to Enhancing Employability Skills and Attributes. *Active Learning in Higher Education*, 15: 39–51.

Deeley, S J and Bovill, C (2017) Staff-Student Partnership in Assessment: Enhancing Assessment Literacy Through Democratic Practices. *Assessment and Evaluation in Higher Education*, 42: 463–77.

Delpish, A, Holmes, A, Knight-McKenna, M, Mihans, R, Darby, A, King, K and Felten, P (2010) Equalizing Voices: Student-Faculty Partnership in Course Design. In Werder, C and Otis, M (eds) *Engaging Student Voices in the Study of Teaching and Learning.* Sterling: Stylus.

Dewey, J (1916) *Democracy and Education: An Introduction to the Philosophy of Education.* New York: The Macmillan Company.

DiSalvo, B, Yip, J, Bonsignore, E and DiSalvo, C (eds) (2017) *Participatory Design for Learning: Perspectives from Practice and Research.* Abingdon: Routledge.

Drummond, T and Shea Owens, K S (2010) Capturing Students' Learning. In Werder C and Otis M (eds) *Engaging Student Voices in The Study of Teaching and Learning.* Sterling: Stylus.

Ecclestone, K and Hayes, D (2019) *The Dangerous Rise of Therapeutic Education.* London: Routledge.

Fawns, T Aitken, G and Jones, D (2019) Online Learning as Embodied, Socially Meaningful Experience. *Postdigital Science and Education*, 1: 293–397. [online] Available at: link.springer.com/article/10.1007/s42438-019-00048-9 (accessed 12 January 2020).

Felten, P (2017) Emotions and Partnership. *International Journal for Students as Partners*, 1: 1–5. [online] Available at: mulpress.mcmaster.ca/ijsap/article/view/3070 (accessed 12 January 2020).

Felten, P, Gardner, J N, Schroeder, C C, Lambert, L and Barefoot, B (2016) *The Undergraduate Experience: Focusing Institutions on What Matters Most.* San Francisco: Jossey Bass.

Felten, P and Lambert, L M (2020) *Relationship-Rich Education: How Human Connections Drive Success in College.* Baltimore, MD: Johns Hopkins University Press.

Fielding, M (1999) Radical Collegiality: Affirming Teaching as an Inclusive Professional Practice. *Australian Educational Researcher*, 26: 1–34.

Fielding, M (2001) Students as Radical Agents of Change. *Journal of Educational Change*, 2: 123–1.

Finkel, D L (2000) *Teaching With Your Mouth Shut.* Portsmouth: Heinemann.

Fisher, D, Frey, N, Quaglia, R J, Smith, D and Lande, L L (2018) *Engagement by Design: Creating Learning Environments Where Students Thrive.* Thousand Oaks, CA: Corwin.

Freeman, S, Eddy, S l, McDonough, M, Smith, M K, Okoroafor, N, Jordt, H and Wenderoth, M P (2014) Active Learning Increases Student Performance in Science, Engineering and Mathematics. *Proceedings of the National Academy of Sciences of the USA*, 111: 8410–15.

Freire, P (2003) From Pedagogy of the Oppressed. In Darder, A, Baltodano, M and Torres, R D (eds) *The Critical Pedagogy Reader*. New York: Routledge.

Freire, P (1993) *Pedagogy of the Oppressed* (revised edition). London: Penguin.

Gibbs, G (2012) *Implications of 'Dimensions of Quality' in a Market Environment*. York: Higher Education Academy.

Gibbs, G (2010) *Dimensions of Quality*. York: Higher Education Academy.

Giroux, H A (1983) *Theory and Resistance in Education: A Pedagogy for the Opposition*. London: Heinemann.

Gozemba, P A (2002) Aloha 'Aina. In De Los Reyes, E and Gozemba, P A (eds) *Pockets of Hope: How Students and Teachers Change the World*. London: Bergin and Garvey.

Gozemba, P A (2002) Crossing the Bridge: Peer Education and Mediation. In De Los Reyes, E and Gozemba, P A (eds) *Pockets of Hope: How Students and Teachers Change the World*. London: Bergin and Garvey.

Greer, A (nd) *Increasing Inclusivity in the Classroom*. Vanderbilt University. [online] Available at: https://cft.vanderbilt.edu/guides-sub-pages/increasing-inclusivity-in-the-classroom/ (accessed 13 January 2020).

Healey, M, Flint, A and Harrington, K (2014) *Students as Partners in Learning and Teaching in Higher Education*. York: Higher Education Academy.

Heidegger, M (1968) *What is Called Thinking?* London: Harper and Row.

Heron, J (1992) The Politics of Facilitation: Balancing Facilitator Authority and Learning Autonomy. In Mulligan, J and Griffin, C (eds) *Empowerment Through Experiential Learning: Explorations of Good Practice*. London: Kogan Page.

hooks, b (1994) *Teaching to Transgress: Education as the Practice of Freedom*. New York: Routledge.

Huxham, M, Scoles, J, Green, U, Purves, S, Welsh, Z and Gray, A (2017) 'Observation has Set in': Comparing Students and Peers as Reviewers of Teaching. *Assessment and Evaluation in Higher Education*, 42: 887–99.

Huxham, M, Hunter, M, McIntyre, A, Shilland, R and McArthur, J (2015) Student and Teacher Co-Navigation of a Course: Following the Natural Lines of Academic Enquiry. *Teaching in Higher Education*, 20: 530–41.

Illich, I (2004) *Deschooling Society* (reprint). London: Marion Boyers.

Iversen, A-M and Stavnskaer Pedersen, A (2017) Co-Creating Knowledge: Students and Teachers Together in a Field of Emergence. In Chemi, T and Krogh, L (eds) *Co-Creation in Higher Education: Students and Educators Preparing Creatively and Collaboratively to the Challenge of the Future*. Rotterdam: Sense.

Jarvis, J and Clark, K (2020) *Conversations to Change Teaching*. St Albans: Critical Publishing.

Kandiko Howson, C (2016) Tef: Don't Equate Contact Hours with Teaching Quality. *The Guardian*, 23 November. [online] Available at: www.theguardian.com/higher-education-network/2016/nov/23/tef-dont-equate-contact-hours-with-teaching-quality (accessed 12 January 2020).

Keller, G (2014) *Transforming a College: The Story of a Little-Known College's Strategic Climb to National Distinction* (updated edition). Baltimore, MD: John Hopkins University Press.

Kenny, M (2019) *Student-Staff Co-Creation of a Course: Understanding Gender in the Contemporary World*. Teaching Matters blog, 10 January, University of Edinburgh. [online] Available at: www.teaching-matters-blog.ed.ac.uk/student-staff-co-creation-of-a-course-understanding-gender-in-the-contemporary-world/ (accessed 12 January 2020).

Komarraju, M, Musulkin, S and Bhattacharya, G (2010) Role of Student-Faculty Interactions in Developing College Students' Academic Self-Concept, Motivation, and Achievement. *Journal of College Student Development*, 51: 332–42.

Kostenius, C and Bergmark, U (2016) The Power of Appreciation: Promoting Schoolchildren's Health Literacy. *Health Education*, 116: 611–26.

Kuh, G D and Hu, S (2001) The Effects of Student-Faculty Interaction in the 1990s. *The Review of Higher Education*, 24: 309–32.

Kuh, G, Kinzie, J, Schuh, J H, Whitt, E J and associates (2005) *Student Success in College: Creating Conditions That Matter.* San Francisco: Jossey Bass.

Kuh, G, O'Donnell, K and Schneider, C G (2017) HIPs at Ten. *Change: The Magazine of Higher Learning*, 49: 8–16.

Lamport, M A (1993) Student-Faculty Informal Interaction and the Effect on College Student Outcomes: A Review of the Literature. *Adolescence*, 28: 971–90.

Levy, D, Svoronos, T and Klinger, M (2018) Two Stage Examinations: Can Examinations be More Formative Experiences? *Active Learning in Higher Education.* [online] Available at: doi.org/10.1177/1469787418801668 (accessed 12 January 2020).

Long, L (1977) *The Effects of Pre-Teaching Teacher Interaction Style on Student Achievement.* Washington DC: Catholic University of America.

Lubicz-Nawrocka, T (2016) *Co-Creation of the Curriculum and Social Justice: Changing the Nature of Student-Teacher Relationships in Higher Education.* Lancaster, UK. Paper presented at Higher Education Close-Up (HECU) Conference, 18–20 July. [online] Available at: www.lancaster.ac.uk/fass/events/hecu8/abstracts/lubicz-nawrocka.htm (accessed 12 January 2020).

Lubicz-Nawrocka, T (2020) *An Exploration of How Curriculum Co-Creation Advances Student and Staff Aims for Scottish Higher Education.* Unpublished PhD thesis, University of Edinburgh.

MacFarlane, B (2004) *Teaching with Integrity: The Ethics of Higher Education Practice.* Abingdon: Routledge.

McCluskey, G (2018) Restorative Approaches in Schools: Current Practices and Future Directions. In Deakin, J, Taylor, E and Kupchik, A (eds) *The Palgrave International Handbook of School Discipline, Surveillance and Social Control.* Basingstoke: Palgrave.

McDaniel, B L (2010) Between Strangers and Soul Mates: Care and Moral Dialogue. In Bingham, C and Sidorkin, A M (eds) *No Education Without Relation.* New York: Peter Lang Publishing.

McWilliam, E (2008) Unlearning How to Teach. *Innovations in Education and Teaching International*, 45: 263–9.

Mann, S J (2001) Alternative Perspectives on the Student Experience: Alienation and Engagement. *Studies in Higher Education*, 26: 7–19.

Manor, C, Bloch-Schulman, S, Flannery, K and Felten, P (2010) Foundations of Student-Faculty Partnerships in the Scholarship of Teaching and Learning. In Werder, C and Otis, M (eds) *Engaging Student Voices in the Study of Teaching and Learning.* Sterling: Stylus.

Marquis, E, Jayaratnam, A, Mishra, A and Rybkina, K (2018) I Feel Like Some Students are Better Connected: Students' Perspectives on Applying for Extracurricular Partnership Opportunities. *International Journal for Students As Partners*, 2: 64–81. [online] Available at: doi.org/10.15173/ijsap.v2i1.3300 (accessed 12 January 2020).

Mayhew, M J, Rockenbach, A N, Bowman, N A, Seifert, T A, Wolniak, G C, Pascarella, E T and Terenzini, P T (2016) *How College Affects Students. Volume 3: 21st Century Evidence that Higher Education Works.* San Francisco: Jossey Bass.

Mercer-Mapstone, L and Bovill, C (2019) Equity and Diversity in Institutional Approaches to Student-Staff Partnership Schemes in Higher Education. *Studies in Higher Education.*[online] Available at: www.tandfonline.com/doi/full/10.1080/03075079.2019.1620721 (accessed 12 January 2020).

Mercer-Mapstone, L, Dvorakova, S L, Matthews, K E, Abbot, S, Cheng, B, Felten, P, Knorr, C, Marquis, E, Shammas, R and Swaim, K (2017) A Systematic Literature Review of Students as Partners in Higher Education. *International Journal for Students as Partners*, 1. [online] Available at: doi.org/10.15173/ijsap.v1i1.3119 (accessed 12 January 2020).

Mercer-Mapstone, L, Islam, M and Reid, T (2019) Are We Just Engaging 'The Usual Suspects'? Challenges in and Practical Strategies for Supporting Equity and Diversity in Student–Staff Partnership Initiatives. *Teaching in Higher Education.* [online] Available at: www.tandfonline.com/doi/full/10.1080/13562517.2019.1655396 (accessed 12 January 2020).

Michael, J (2006) Where's the Evidence that Active Learning Works? *Advances in Physiology Education*, 30: 159–67.

Mihans, R, Long, D and Felten, P (2008) Power and Expertise: Student–Faculty Collaboration in Course Design and the Scholarship of Teaching and Learning. *International Journal for the Scholarship of Teaching and Learning*, 2: 1–9.

Moore-Cherry, N, Healey, R, Nicholson, D T and Andrews, W (2016) Inclusive Partnership: Enhancing Student Engagement in Geography. *Journal of Geography in Higher Education*, 40: 84–103.

Newell Decyk, B, Murphy, M, Currier, D G and Long, D T (2010) Challenges and Caveats. In Werder, C and Otis, M (eds) *Engaging Student Voices in the Study of Teaching and Learning.* Sterling: Stylus.

Noddings, N (1984) *Caring: A Relational Approach to Ethics and Moral Education.* Berkeley: University of California Press.

Noddings, N (1992) *The Challenge to Care in Schools: An Alternative Approach to Education.* New York: Teachers College Press.

Noddings, N (2010) Foreword. In Bingham, C and Sidorkin, A M (eds) *No Education Without Relation.* New York: Peter Lang Publishing.

Otis, M M and Hammond, J D (2010) Participatory Action Research as a Rationale for Student Voices in the Scholarship of Teaching and Learning. In Werder, C and Otis, M (eds) *Engaging Student Voices in the Study of Teaching and Learning.* Sterling: Stylus.

Palmer, P J (1983) *To Know as we are Known: Education as a Spiritual Journey.* San Francisco: Harper.

Palmer, P J (1998) *The Courage to Teach: Exploring the Inner Landscape of a Teacher's Life.* San Francisco: Jossey Bass.

Pascarella, E and Terenzini, P (1978) Student Faculty Informal Relationships and Freshman Year Educational Outcomes. *Journal of Educational Research*, 71: 183–9.

Pascarella, E and Terenzini, P (2005) *How College Affects Students. Volume 2: A Third Decade of Research.* San Francisco: Jossey Bass.

Pinar, W F (1981) The Reconceptualization of Curriculum Studies. In Giroux, H A, Penna, A N and Pinar, W F (eds) *Curriculum and Instruction Alternatives in Education.* Berkeley: McCutchen Publishing.

Pitt, E and Winstone, N (2018) The Impact of Anonymous Marking on Students' Perceptions of Fairness, Feedback and Relationships with Lecturers. *Assessment and Evaluation in Higher Education*, 43: 1183–93.

Plevin, R (2017) *Connect with your Students: How to Build Positive Teacher-Student Relationships – The #1 Secret to Effective Classroom Management.* Amazon.com: Needs Focused Teaching/Life Raft Media Ltd.

Quinlan, K M (2016) How Emotion Matters in Four Key Relationships in Teaching and Learning in Higher Education. *College Teaching*, 64: 101–11.

Queens' University (nd) *Expanding the Conservations: Developing Inclusisve Pedagogy Models.* [online] Available at: http://queensu.ca/equity/EDIonline (accessed 13 January 2020).

Rogers, C and Freiberg, H J (1994) *Freedom to Learn* (3rd ed). New York: Macmillan Publishing.

Romano, R M (2010) Reading Relations. In Bingham, C and Sidorkin, A M (eds) *No Education Without Relation.* New York: Peter Lang Publishing.

Roxå, T and Mårtensson, K (2009) Significant Conversations and Significant Networks – Exploring the Backstage of the Teaching Arena. *Studies in Higher Education*, 34: 547–59.

Ryan, A and Tilbury, D (2013) *Flexible Pedagogies: New Pedagogical Ideas.* York: Higher Education Academy.

Scheck, D C and Bizio, S (1977) Students' Perceptions of the Ideal Professor. *College Student Journal*, 11: 335–42.

Schwartz, H L (2019) *Connected Teaching: Relationship, Power and Mattering in Higher Education*. Sterling: Stylus.

Scoles, J, Huxham, M, Sinclair, K, Lewis, C, Jung, J and Dougall, E (2019) The Other Side of a Magic Mirror: Exploring Collegiality in Student and Staff Partnership Work. *Teaching in Higher Education*. [online] Available at: www.tandfonline.com/doi/full/10.1080/13562517.2019.1677588 (accessed 12 January 2020).

Shor, I (1992) *Empowering Education: Critical Teaching for Social Change*. London: University of Chicago Press.

Shrewsbury, C M (1987) What is Feminist Pedagogy? *Women's Studies Quarterly*, 15: 6–14.

Sims, S, King, S, Lowe, T and El-Hakim, Y (2016) Evaluating Partnership and Impact in the First Year of the Student Fellows Scheme. *Journal of Educational Innovation, Partnership and Change* 2. [online] Available at: journals.studentengagement.org.uk/index.php/studentchangeagents/article/view/257/2832 (accessed 12 January 2020).

Thayer-Bacon, B J (2010) Personal and Social Relations in Education. In Bingham, C and Sidorkin, A M (eds) *No Education Without Relation*. New York: Peter Lang Publishing.

Theophilides, C and Terenzini, P C (1981) The Relation Between Nonclassroom Contact with Faculty and Students' Perceptions of Instructional Quality. *Research in Higher Education*, 15: 255–69.

Thomas, L (2012) *Building Student Engagement and Belonging in Higher Education at a Time of Change: Final Report from the What Works? Student Retention and Success Programme*. London: Paul Hamlyn Foundation/ HEFCE/Higher Education Academy.

University of Edinburgh (2019) *Near Future Teaching. Co-designing a Values-based Vision for Digital Education at the University of Edinburgh*. Edinburgh: University of Edinburgh.

Victoria University (2019) *First Year College*. Melbourne, Australia: Victoria University. [online] Available at: www.vu.edu.au/about-vu/our-teaching-colleges-schools/first-year-college (accessed 12 January 2020).

Weiman, C E, Rieger, G W and Heiner, C E (2014) Physics Exams that Promote Collaborative Learning. *The Physics Teacher*, 52. [online] Available at: aapt.scitation.org/doi/10.1119/1.4849159 (accessed 12 January 2020).

Werder, C, Ware, L, Thomas, C and Skogsburg, E (2010) Students in Parlor Talk on Teaching and Learning. In Werder, C and Otis, M (eds) *Engaging Student Voices in the Study of Teaching and Learning*. Sterling: Stylus.

Williamson, M (2020) *Personal email communication*. 11 January.

Willis, P (1977) *Learning to Labour: How Working Class Kids get Working Class Jobs*. Aldershot: Ashgate Publishing.

Wilson, S, Meskhidze, H, Felten, P, Bloch Shulman, S, Phillips, J, Lockard, C and McGowan, S (2020) From Novelty to Norm: Moving Beyond Exclusion and the Double Justification Problem in Student-Faculty Partnerships. In Mercer-Mapstone, L and Abbot, S (eds) *The Power of Partnerships: Students, Staff and Faculty Revolutionising Higher Education*. Elon: Elon University Center for Engaged Learning. [online] Available at: www.centerforengagedlearning.org/books/power-of-partnership/ (accessed 15 January 2020).

Wolf-Wendel, L, Ward, K and Kinzie, J (2009) A Tangled Web of Terms: The Overlap and Unique Contribution of Involvement, Engagement, and Integration to Understanding College Student Success. *Journal of College Student Development*, 50: 407–28.

Yahinaaw/Grant, A (2019) T'aats'iigang: Stuffing a Jar Full. *International Journal for Students as Partners*, 3: 6–10. [online] Available at: doi.org/10.15173/ijsap.v3i2.4081 (accessed 12 January 2020).

Index